Origami in King Arthur's Court

Origami in King Arthur's Court

An Adventure in Folding by Lew Rozelle

St. Martin's Griffin
New York

I would like to thank my editors, Jill McFarlane for beginning the arduous task of editing the manuscript for publication and Joy Chang for seeing the book to final printing. Special thanks are in order to Samuel Randlett for editing the drawings and instructions and his many suggestions that have been immeasurably appreciated.

Design by Lew Rozelle

Library of Congress Cataloging-in-Publication Data

Rozelle, Lew.
    Origami in King Arthur's court : an adventure in folding / by Lew
    Rozelle. — 1st ed.
        p.   cm.
    ISBN 0-312-15619-7
    1. Origami.   2. Knights and knighthood in art.   3. Castles in art.
    I. Title.
    TT870.R68 1997
    736'.982 — dc21   97-5636
                                                                   CIP

First St. Martin's Griffin Edition: August 1997

10 9 8 7 6 5 4 3 2 1

Introduction

This book is different in two ways from any origami book found on the market today. First, the models are simple enough that if you have mastered the Japanese crane or can fold a bird base, you can complete many of the most complex models. Second, the book is not a collection of unrelated models; it is rather a complete storybook. The story here is the legend of King Arthur, and all of its characters can be folded: King Arthur, Guinevere, Merlin, Lancelot. Different castles can be invented and built. There are as many ways to fold the cast of characters as the imagination can dream up. Teachers can use the models not only as a learning experience in following instructions, but also to demonstrate what life might have been like during the Middle Ages.

Before you begin to fold the models in this book, I strongly recommend that you look at the section on proportional paper. I started developing what I call proportional origami as a way of creating complex origami figures from extremely simple models. I began making the castles and Merlin's tower from simple boxes that were the right dimensions to fit together like building blocks. They needed a means of fastening them together so that they would not fall apart, so I added a system of flaps and pockets to the boxes.

Once I designed and built the castles, I wanted to fill them with the characters and objects I had read about as a child. To be truly proportional, the castles would have to be very large or the people and other figures would have to be extremely small, probably too small to fold easily. Since I had used 8″ squares to make the castle parts, I decided to use 8″ as my base paper for the other models also. This makes the human figures somewhat large for the castles, but results in pleasing proportions. As I folded the characters, I developed a system for keeping all the models in proportion while using any base paper.

The castles and tower had been fashioned from bond typing paper and colored butcher paper, but animals and people were a different story. These could not be folded from stiff bond paper. Instead, I began making my own paper by laminating foil-backed paper with tissue paper. This worked extremely well for fashioning the small arms and legs of the figures. Next, I found a way to laminate papers so that, once folded, different parts of the models would have the appropriate colors and textures. Experimentation is part of the fun and I have suggested many ways that you can continue to develop further your own cast of characters.

I hope you enjoy folding these paper models as much as I have.

Lew Rozelle

Contents

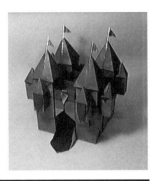

A Knight in Shining Armor

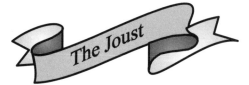

The Joust

Merlin's Domain

The Realm of Camelot

The Royal Hunt

The Adventure Begins

Proportional Origami

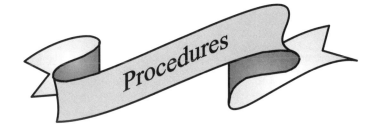

- - - - - -   Valley Fold

· - · - · - · -   Mountain Fold

- - - - ✄   Cut

⟶   Fold in Front

⟶   Fold Behind

⟹   Open Out

⟹   Enlarged View

⌁⟶   Pleat

⟶   Turn Model Over

⟶   Fold Over and Over

⟋   Fold and Unfold

▶   Sink or Push In

●   Watch This Spot

○   Hold Here

International symbols for folding paper

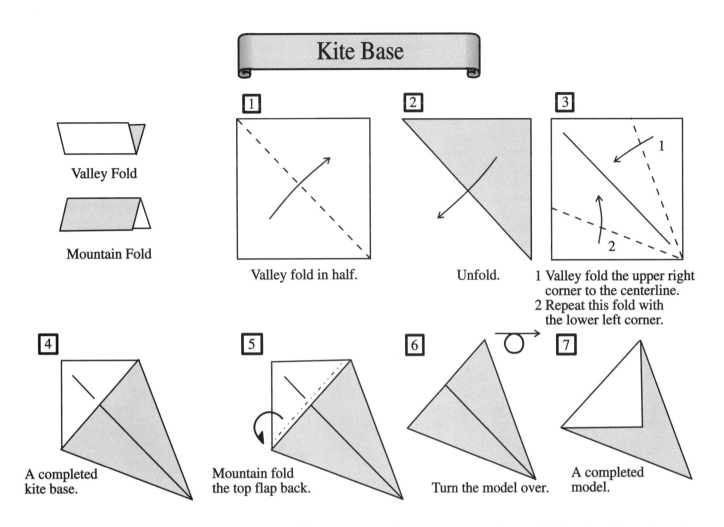

Kite Base

Valley Fold

Mountain Fold

1 Valley fold in half.

2 Unfold.

3
1 Valley fold the upper right corner to the centerline.
2 Repeat this fold with the lower left corner.

4 A completed kite base.

5 Mountain fold the top flap back.

6 Turn the model over.

7 A completed model.

If you are already an accomplished paper folder, you may skip this section and start folding the fairy tale castle. Otherwise, let's begin by learning to fold the basic models.

Use any square piece of paper that is colored on one side and white on the other. Place the colored side of the paper down on a flat surface or hold the paper so that the colored side is away from you. Step 1 shows what your paper should look like. Notice that the paper is not shaded. The color is on the opposite side. It is important for you to follow each drawing exactly as it is shown in the book. Notice the dashed line on the drawing. The broken lines in the drawing tell you what kind of fold to make. The dashed line indicates a valley fold. Fold the paper in the direction of the arrow, so that the corners are perfectly even, and then crease the paper, making a fold.

Now look at step 2. Your paper should look like this if you folded correctly. The drawing is of a triangle with only color showing. The instructions at the bottom of a drawing tell you what to do in each step; in step 2, unfold the paper. Step 3 shows your paper open again, and no color is showing. There are two dashed lines, each with a number. The fold you made in step 1 is now a line on the drawing. It is the crease line that runs diagonally along the center of the paper. It's called a centerline. The instructions in step 3 tell you to fold the corners to the centerline. Look at step 4 as you fold and you can see where to line up the edge of your paper. Step 4 shows how your paper should look. This drawing is of a kite base, which is used in making Merlin's cloak.

Step 5 is a little different. The folding line is made up of dots and dashes, indicating a mountain fold. A mountain fold may also be indicated by a curved arrow with a different point on the end. You make a mountain fold by folding the paper back away from you, sometimes down or even up into a model, thereby forming an edge on the paper. Step 6 shows what the paper should look like. The instruction tells you to turn the model over. The symbol for this process is the circle and arrow above the drawing. When you see this symbol, it means to turn the model over for the next step. Step 7 shows the completed model on the reverse side.

Fish Base

1. Valley fold to the centerline. Unfold the paper.

2. Valley fold to the centerline. Unfold the paper.

3. Valley fold the sides to the centerline to form a separate flap.

4. Repeat steps 1-3 on the remaining half.

5. A completed fish base.

An enlarged view of the finished model.

The drawings above show how to fold a fish base. It's simple to fold and very useful in making small models such as the knight's shield.

Step 1 contains a simple valley fold. Step 2 shows the same fold but in the opposite direction. Step 3 is a little more complicated. Fold both flaps down to the centerline at the same time, making a valley fold where indicated. When you do this, you will form a small flap in the center. Don't worry if your small flap points in the opposite direction than that shown in step 4. Simply fold this small flap so it looks like the drawing. These folds together are called a rabbit ear fold.

Step 4 shows how to fold the opposite side of the paper using steps 1-3. If your model looks like step 5, you have successfully made a fish base. Step 5 shows the finished fish base drawing and an enlarged view of the model. It is sometimes necessary to enlarge part of a drawing to make it easier to see the folds.

Look at the small drawing at the bottom of the page. Once you know how to make a rabbit ear fold, this is all the information you will need.

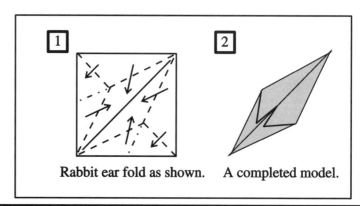

1. Rabbit ear fold as shown.

2. A completed model.

Waterbomb Base

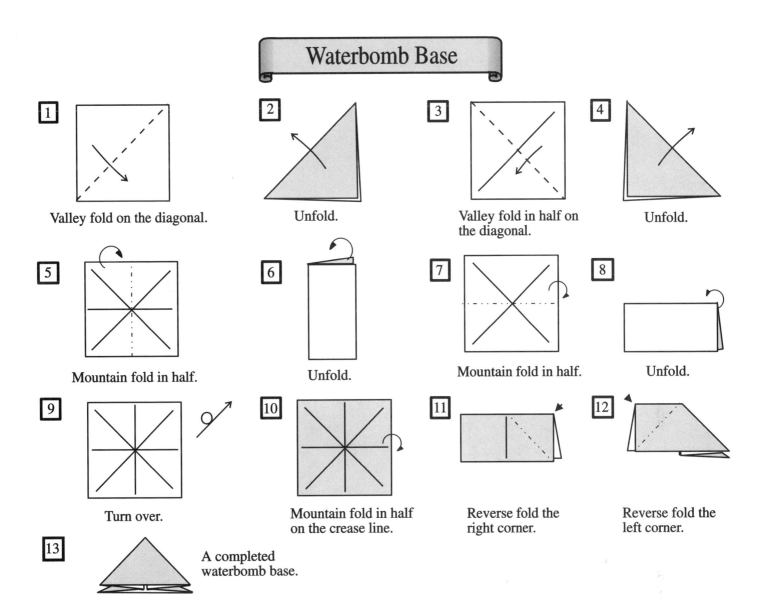

1 Valley fold on the diagonal.

2 Unfold.

3 Valley fold in half on the diagonal.

4 Unfold.

5 Mountain fold in half.

6 Unfold.

7 Mountain fold in half.

8 Unfold.

9 Turn over.

10 Mountain fold in half on the crease line.

11 Reverse fold the right corner.

12 Reverse fold the left corner.

13 A completed waterbomb base.

The drawings above show how to fold a waterbomb base. Begin with a square piece of paper color side down. Step 1 tells you to valley fold the paper on the diagonal and shows the direction to make the fold. It is very important when folding the waterbomb base to be as precise as you can. The edges of the paper must be lined up exactly. Step 2 shows what the paper looks like after you have made the fold. It also tells you to unfold the paper. Step 3 tells you to make another valley fold and the direction to fold. Step 4 shows the paper after the fold and tells you to unfold the paper again. In later drawings, these two steps of folding and unfolding are included in one step. I have separated these two procedures for clarity.

Steps 5 and 6 tell you to make a mountain fold, the direction, and to unfold the paper. Notice that when you unfold the paper there is no color. Since you made a mountain fold, you should bring the paper back to the same side you began the fold. Again in steps 7 and 8 you mountain fold the paper and unfold it. Step 9 shows the paper with all the creases you have made so far. In step 9 you can now turn the paper over. Step 10 takes advantage of the folds you made in the first steps. The paper is folded along the same fold line you made in step 7.

Step 11 is a new fold. Look at the direction of the folds in the paper. There is a small arrowhead in the drawing. Push the edge of the paper near the arrow down inside the paper. The folds will allow you to do this easily. This fold is called a reverse fold because you are changing a mountain fold into a valley fold. Look at step 12. Your paper should look like this. In step 12, you repeat the same reverse fold on the opposite side of the paper. If you have made the folds properly, your model should look like step 13.

The waterbomb base is used to make parts of the castles and objects rather than figures of animate objects.

Bird Base

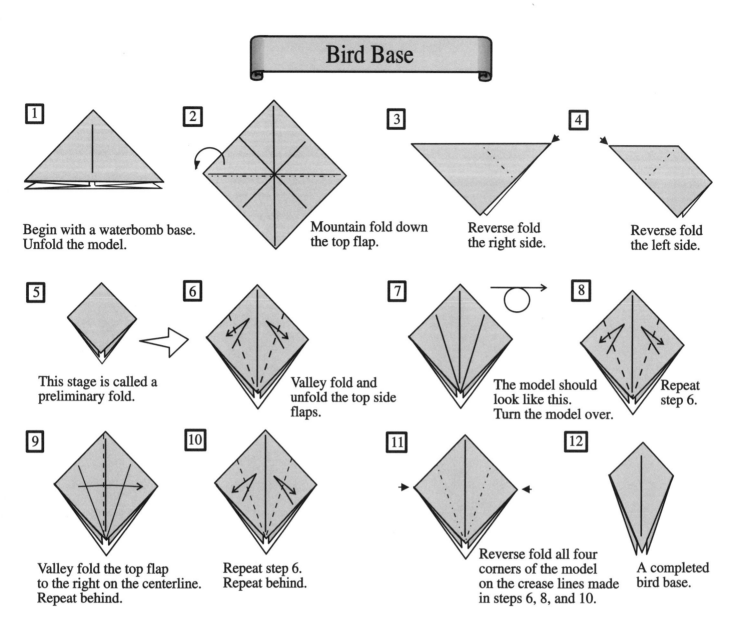

1 Begin with a waterbomb base. Unfold the model.

2 Mountain fold down the top flap.

3 Reverse fold the right side.

4 Reverse fold the left side.

5 This stage is called a preliminary fold.

6 Valley fold and unfold the top side flaps.

7 The model should look like this. Turn the model over.

8 Repeat step 6.

9 Valley fold the top flap to the right on the centerline. Repeat behind.

10 Repeat step 6. Repeat behind.

11 Reverse fold all four corners of the model on the crease lines made in steps 6, 8, and 10.

12 A completed bird base.

I will show you how to fold a bird base in which all the edges of the paper will be perfectly aligned. Begin in step 1 with a waterbomb base. Unfold the base so that the color side is up. Turn the paper so that it looks like the drawing in step 2. Step 2 consists of mountain folding the paper on the diagonal. Step 3 shows how the paper should look and requires that you reverse fold the right flap into the model. This is the same process of folding you did to make the waterbomb base. Step 4 tells you to reverse fold the left side of the paper in the same way. Normally, these two steps would appear in one drawing, but for clarity I have separated the two. Your model should look like step 5. If you have folded the paper properly, you will not be able to see the edges shown at the bottom of the drawing. (They are there to help you see if you folded the model properly.)

Step 6 shows you a new symbol. This symbol tells you to fold and unfold the paper. First valley fold the near flaps to the centerline and crease the fold. Now unfold the paper so that it looks like step 7. Step 7 shows how the model should look and tells you to turn the model over. Step 8 tells you to repeat the folds that you made in step 6, folding only the top layer of the paper. Step 9 tells you to valley fold the near left flap over to the right. It also has you repeat this procedure on the reverse side of the model so that there are two flaps on each side of the centerline. Step 10 tells you to repeat step 6 again along the same creases. You do this on both sides of the paper. These folds help to even the edges of the paper and allow you to reverse fold the flaps in step 11. Step 11 has you reverse fold all four of the flaps into the model. If you have folded the model correctly and carefully, you will have a finished bird base. All the edges of the model should be very even. There should be no white showing on any of the flaps of paper.

Common Folds

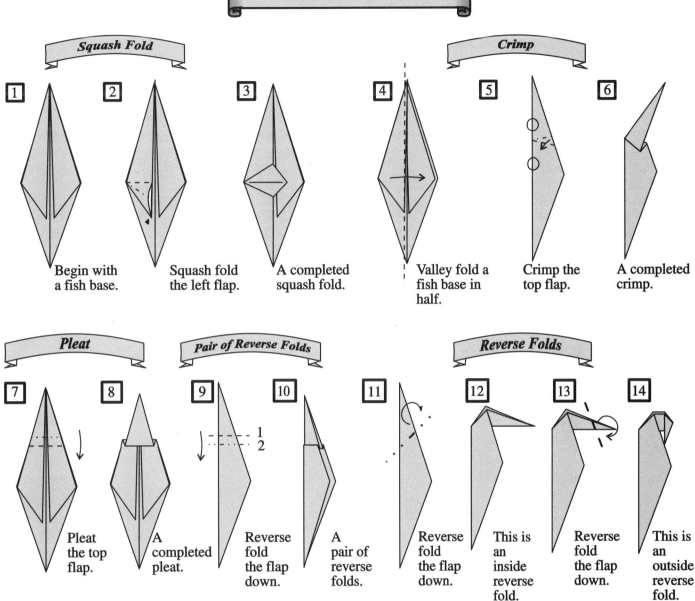

Squash Fold

1 Begin with a fish base.

2 Squash fold the left flap.

3 A completed squash fold.

Crimp

4 Valley fold a fish base in half.

5 Crimp the top flap.

6 A completed crimp.

Pleat

7 Pleat the top flap.

8 A completed pleat.

Pair of Reverse Folds

9 Reverse fold the flap down.

10 A pair of reverse folds.

Reverse Folds

11 Reverse fold the flap down.

12 This is an inside reverse fold.

13 Reverse fold the flap down.

14 This is an outside reverse fold.

The drawings above show how to make four common folds. Steps 1–3 illustrate a squash fold. Step 1 begins with a fish base. Step 2 shows where to make a valley and mountain fold. In step 2, simply lift up the center flap and open it up. Press down on the flap so that the point of the flap is horizontal to the centerline, and press (squash) the flap flat.

Steps 4–6 illustrate a crimp. Step 4 is simply valley folding the model in half. Step 5 has a new symbol. The small round circles tell you where to hold the model while you make the fold. By making the valley and mountain folds in the drawing as you hold on to the model, you will form a crimp that looks like step 6.

Steps 7–8 show how to make a simple pleat. Valley fold the top of the paper down, then fold part of the flap back up. You may make the mountain fold first if you wish. Steps 9–10 show how to make a pair of reverse folds when the flap is not open.

Steps 11–12 illustrate an inside reverse fold. Mountain fold both sides of the model so that the top point extends out to the right. In the process you will make a mountain fold into a valley fold (thus reversing the fold). Steps 13 –14 show an outside reverse fold. Since you are working with a flap that is valley folded, when you reverse fold this flap you will turn the valley fold into a mountain fold. The only way you can accomplish this is by folding the paper on the outside of the flap. You will use the outside reverse fold to make the heads of the human figures.

Laminated Paper

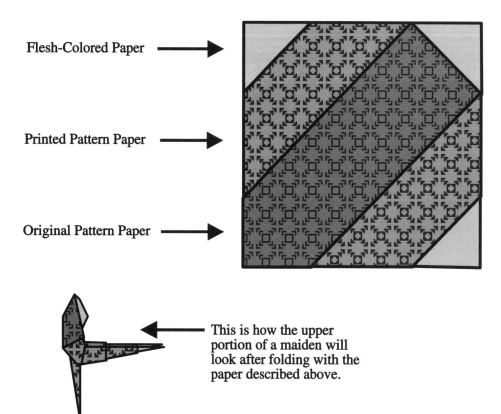

Flesh-Colored Paper ⟶

Printed Pattern Paper ⟶

Original Pattern Paper ⟶

This is how the upper portion of a maiden will look after folding with the paper described above. ⟵

The drawing above is that of a laminated paper. Laminated paper is fairly easy to make and allows you to experiment with colors and textures while making the models in this book.

Laminated paper is made by using a square paper the size you intend to fold. Onto this square, you glue strips of paper of an appropriate color and texture. The example above uses a square paper with a pattern printed on it. Gift wrap is a good example, or you may wish to use origami paper. On the square, you glue flesh-colored paper where the face and hands will be folded. You can figure out exactly where and how much by unfolding a finished model. A different pattern paper is added where the arms and torso will be folded. You may wish to make the maiden's skirt out of the same paper. I have found that crepe paper, when glued to a square of fairly thin paper, makes a very fine texture for a dragon.

REMEMBER! You're not supposed to use glue once you have made your paper, but it is quite acceptable to glue when making the sheet you intend to fold. Try to find a flexible glue, such as *Arleen's Tacky Glue,* that will bend when you fold. Laminated paper has replaced the earlier custom of writing or drawing on paper before folding it. I will give you more ideas on laminated paper as you begin folding the characters in King Arthur's court.

Even if you do not use a laminated paper in your constructions, you can make models look just as they appear in this book. Merlin can be made from black or a dark-colored paper. The knight can be folded from a candy wrapper or a foil-backed paper. Be as creative in the use of paper as you can. The small models such as the hat or cloak can be folded from different-colored papers and added to any of the human figures. You might try to make the upper half of a figure from one color paper and the lower half from a contrasting color. Enjoyment in origami begins with the paper you use to fold.

For clarity of instruction, many of the illustrations in this book show a paper that has color on one side and white on the other, but when not using laminated paper, your origami paper should always have the same color on both sides. Also remember that the given paper sizes are only suggestions. Models can be made from larger paper, but be sure to use proportionally sized paper for all the models in your construction.

Construction Set

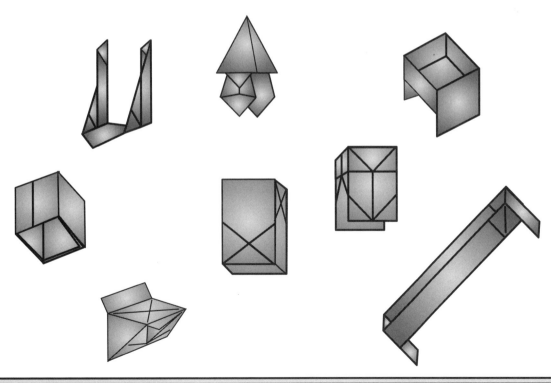

Building Block

Fold the building block from two 8″ square sheets of paper.

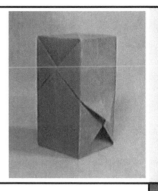

1

Begin with a waterbomb base.
Valley fold (1) top to bottom edge and unfold.
Valley fold (2) each flap to top point and unfold.
Valley fold (3) each flap to centerline and unfold.
Repeat behind.

2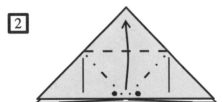

Work only with the near layer.
Lift the bottom edge all the way to the top and squash fold the side flaps to the centerline.
Watch the black dots.
Repeat behind.

3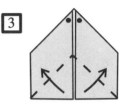

Your paper should look like this.
Valley fold the small corners diagonally upward as shown.
Repeat behind.

4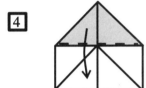

Valley fold down the near top flap.
Repeat behind.

5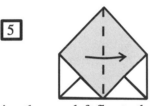

Swing the near left flap to the right.
Repeat behind.

6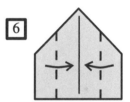

Valley fold the sides to the centerline.
Repeat behind.

7

Valley fold down the top point and unfold.
Repeat behind.

8

Open up the paper from the bottom while pushing down on the top point.
Crease all the folds.

9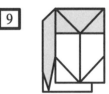

This is a completed half building block.

Make two half building blocks. Slide the rectangular flaps of both models inside each other.

Keep the pointed flaps outside the models as you slide the two half building blocks together.

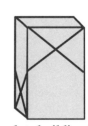

A complete building block.

Sleeve

Fold the sleeve from an 8″ square sheet of paper.

1

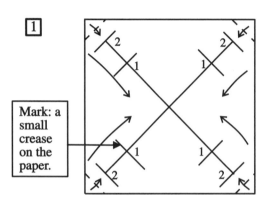

Mark: a small crease on the paper.

Fold the paper in half on each diagonal and unfold.
Valley fold (1) each corner to the center and mark. Unfold.
Valley fold (2) each corner over to mark #1 and make a second mark. Unfold.
Valley fold each corner to mark #2.
Do **not** unfold these corners.

2

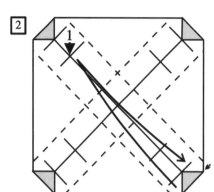

Valley fold a corner edge over the centerline to first crease mark and unfold.
Repeat on the three remaining corners.
Refold the bottom right corner.

3

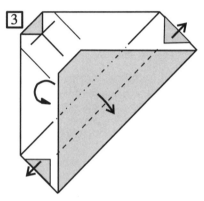

Form in the near colored layer a mountain fold that lies on the crease made in step 2. Then make a valley fold that lies on the diagonal crease of the original square. Unfold the two small corners as shown.

4

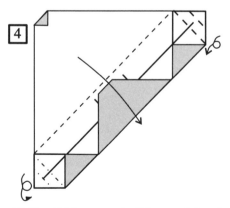

Valley fold one end of the model twice.
Mountain fold the opposite end twice.
Valley fold the top flap along the crease line.

5

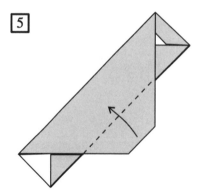

Valley fold the colored flap: the crease should lie along the underlying edge.

6

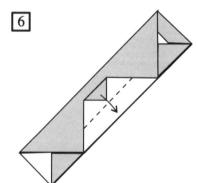

Valley fold the flap to the edge.

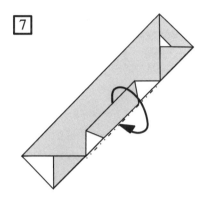

7

Swing the entire flap beyond the edge
and tuck it inside between the colored
layers, like a flap into an envelope.

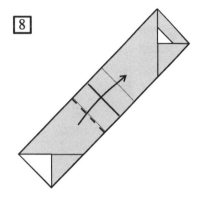

8

Valley fold along crease mark
left by step 2.

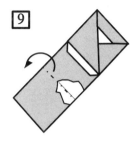

9

Mountain fold the near flap;
this new crease should lie
along the existing crease
formed in the far flap in step 2.
Repeat steps 8–9 on the far flap.

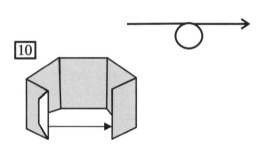

10

Insert the end of the flap inside
the flaps on the opposite side of
the model. When you pull on
the model you should feel the
paper lock together. You may
have to open the inside flaps
slightly to accomplish the step.
Turn the sleeve over.

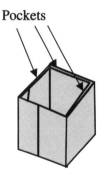

Pockets

A completed sleeve.

Roof

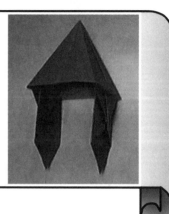

Fold the roof from an 8″ square sheet of paper.

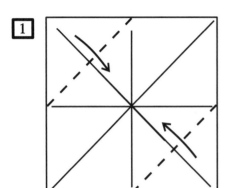

1 Begin with an unfolded waterbomb base. Valley fold opposite corners to the center.

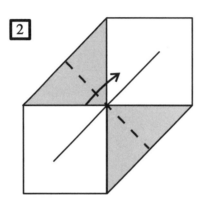

2 Valley fold the paper in half.

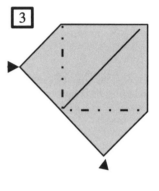

3 Reverse fold opposite corners inward to the centerline.

4 Valley fold the sides to the centerline. Repeat behind.

5 Valley fold the sides to the centerline. Unfold these two folds.

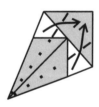

6 Refold step 5 inside the near layer, rolling the white edges inside the colored pockets. Repeat steps 5–6 behind.

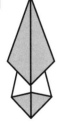

7 Turn your paper to look like this.

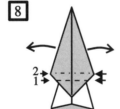

8 Valley fold (1) and mountain fold (2) the flap up inside the unit as shown. Repeat behind, then pull the sides outward.

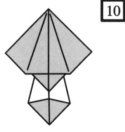

9 Open up the roof from the bottom.

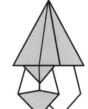

10 The completed roof unit.

Drawbridge

Fold the drawbridge from an 8″ square sheet of paper.

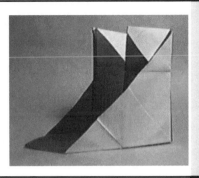

1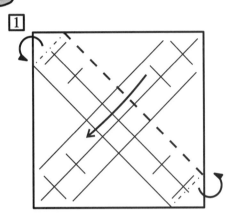

Proceed through step 2 of the sleeve.
Unfold the paper as shown above.
Mountain fold back two corners as shown.
Valley fold down the top flap;
the crease already exists.

2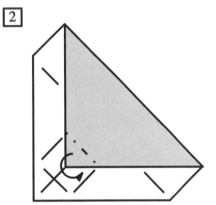

Mountain fold back the small
colored corner where its edges
touch the two central crease lines.

3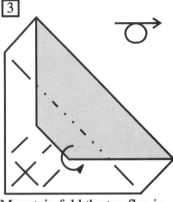

Mountain fold the top flap in
along the crease line.
Turn the model over.

4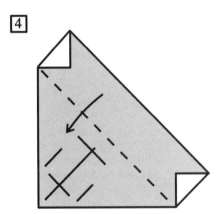

Valley fold along the
existing crease as shown.

5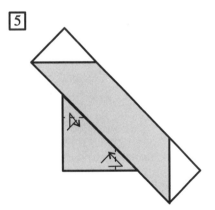

Valley fold and unfold the bottom flap
as shown in the drawing. These folds will
allow the drawbridge to raise and lower.

6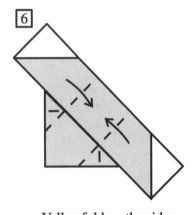

Valley fold up the sides
along the existing creases.

The drawbridge can be made to open
and close by reverse folding the side
flaps up into the folds along the sides
of the drawbridge.

Fold the eight-sided cone from an 8″ square sheet of paper.

1

Begin with a waterbomb base.
Valley fold the top right flap diagonally
about one third the length of the
bottom edge of the paper.

2

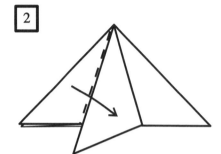

Valley fold the opposite flap
over the top of the flap formed in
step 1. Adjust the angles of the
flaps until each matches the other
exactly.

3

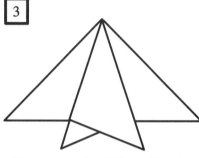

Your paper should look like this.
Repeat steps 1–2 behind.

4

Mountain fold and unfold the near layers.
Valley fold the bottom flaps up
to the crease line.
Repeat behind.

5

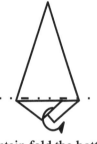

Mountain fold the bottom flaps
up into the pocket just behind them.
Be careful to get both flaps between
the layers.
Repeat behind.

6

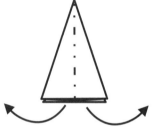

Open out the model from
beneath and flatten it.

7

When the unit is opened it
will form an eight-sided cone.

Tower Top

Fold the tower top from an 8″ square sheet of paper.

1

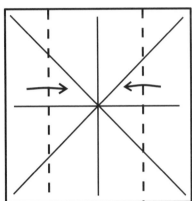

Begin with an unfolded waterbomb base.
Valley fold the side flaps to the centerline.

2

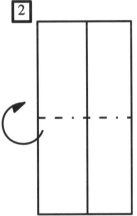

Mountain fold the model
upward in half.

3

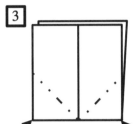

Reverse fold the bottom
corners inward.

4

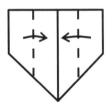

Valley fold the sides in
to the centerline.
Repeat behind.

5

Valley fold the bottom
point upward; unfold.
Repeat behind.

6

Valley fold down the
top flap.
Repeat behind.

7

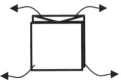

Open up the unit to
form a small box with
side flaps. Crease all the
edges.

8

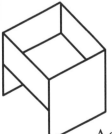

A completed tower top.

Fold the support block from an 8″ square sheet of paper.

1

Start with a waterbomb base.
Valley fold the top point down to
the bottom edge and unfold.
Valley fold the top point down to
the crease line made by the first
valley fold and unfold.

2
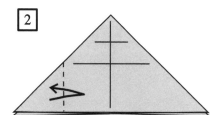

Valley fold the left corner
rightward to the centerline
and unfold.

3
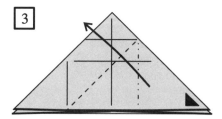

Squash fold the right corner from
the edge of the first crease line
down to where the crease line
intersects the bottom edge.
Watch the black triangle.

4
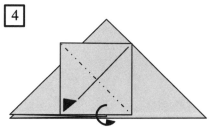

Mountain fold the near layer
inside the top flap.

5
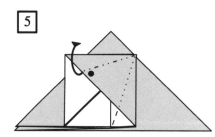

Swivel the upper left corner
clockwise as shown and flatten
the unit.
Watch the black dot.

6
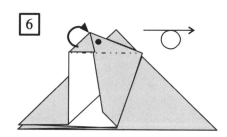

Mountain fold the upper part of
the near top flap to the back.
Turn the paper over.

7
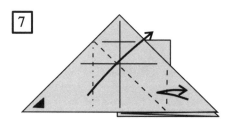

Repeat step 2 on the right side of the
top flap.
Squash fold the left corner from the
edge of the first crease line down to
where the crease line intersects the
bottom edge of the paper.
Watch the black triangle.

8
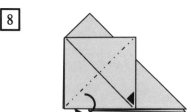

Mountain fold the near layer
inside the top flap.

9
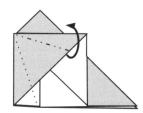

Repeat steps 5 and 6 with the
upper right corner.
Do **not** turn the model over.

 10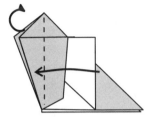

Swing the near right flap all
the way to the left. Then swing
to the right the small central
triangle in the back.

11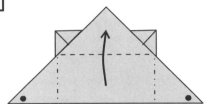

Squash fold the lower corners to
the top.
Watch the black dots.

12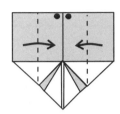

Valley fold the sides of the
near flaps to the centerline.

13

Mountain fold the two central corners
into the pockets behind them.

14

Valley fold the top
flap down.

15

Side view of the
completed support
block.

16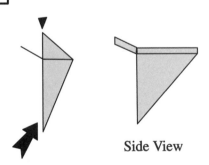

Side View

Open the support block by inserting a finger
into the left of the unit. Push the sides out as
you push down on the top. Look at the finished
unit to the right. It will seem awkward at first
but the unit will begin to take shape as you
open it. Continue to push out the sides and
flatten the top. Pinch all the edges to sharpen
them.

17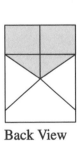

Back View

18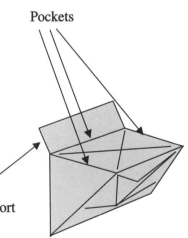

Pockets

This flap is used
to attach the support
block.

Connector

Fold the connector from an 8″ square sheet of paper.

1

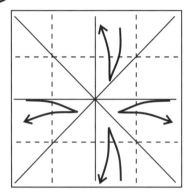

Begin with an unfolded waterbomb base.
Valley fold all the edges to the center and unfold.

2

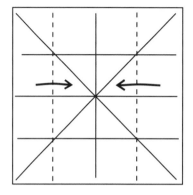

Valley fold the edges to the vertical centerline.

3

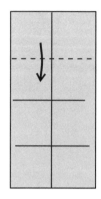

Valley fold the top section down along the existing crease.

4

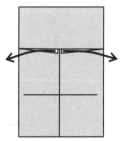

Grasp the two central corners and pull them outward as far as they will go. Flatten the unit.

5

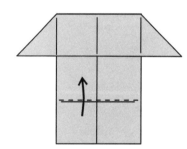

Repeat the actions of steps 3–4 on the bottom.

6

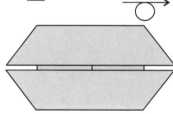

Turn the unit over.

7

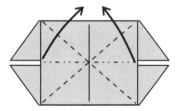

Form the central square into a waterbomb with its point down; the creases already exist.

8

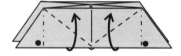

Squash the near corners; watch the black dots.

9

Valley fold the nearest layers diagonally in half.

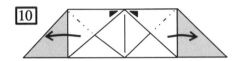

10 Pull the central pockets outward as far as possible; watch the black triangles.

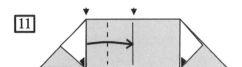

11 Valley fold the white vertical edge of the left flap to the centerline.

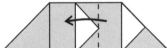

12 Repeat step 6 on the right side of the paper.

13 Mountain fold the near white flap into the triangular pocket hidden just behind it. Repeat steps 8–13 behind.

14 Open out the unit from above and crease all the edges to sharpen them.

Pockets

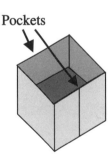

15

Rampart

Fold the rampart from two 8″ square sheets of paper.

1.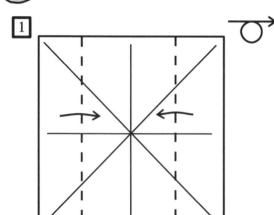

   Begin with an unfolded waterbomb base.
   Valley fold the side flaps to the centerline.
   Turn the unit over.

2.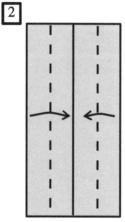

   Valley fold the sides
   to the centerline.

3.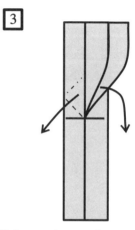

   Pull the top inner edges outward
   and flatten the upper flap downward.
   These inner edges will lie along the
   present horizontal centerline in step 4.

4.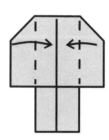

   Valley fold in the sides to the centerline.

5.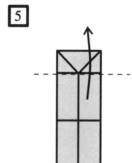

   Valley fold the near layer
   upward as shown.

6.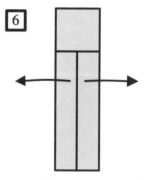

   Open up the unit from the front
   to form an open ended box.

7.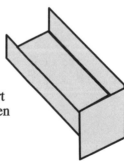

   Half of a rampart
   Fold another, then
   assemble them.

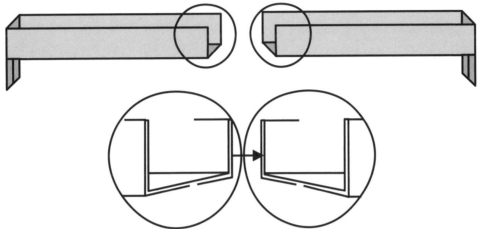

Insert the end of one unit into the end of the second.
Slide the two models together until the rampart is the proper length.

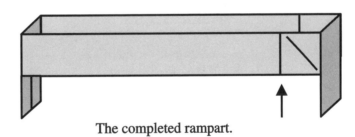

The completed rampart.

Insert the ends of two half ramparts to make a complete rampart that is adjustable in length. The open ends of the ramparts will slide together. After they are joined together, pull them apart far enough to fit over three joined building blocks. The model of Camelot requires that the end of the outside rampart line up with the diagonal folds on the inside rampart.

Arched Block

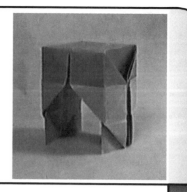

Fold the arched block from an 8″ square sheet of paper.

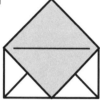

1

Begin with step 5 of the
building block.

2

Valley fold the point up
to the crease line.
Repeat behind.

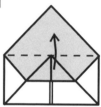

3

Valley fold the flap
along the crease line.
Repeat behind.

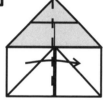

4

Valley fold the near side
in half along the centerline.
Repeat behind.

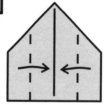

5

Valley fold the sides
to the centerline.
Repeat behind.

6

Valley fold the top
triangle downward; unfold.
Repeat behind.

7

Open up the finished
model. Crease the edges
of the folds.

The completed arched block.

The Fairy Tale Castle

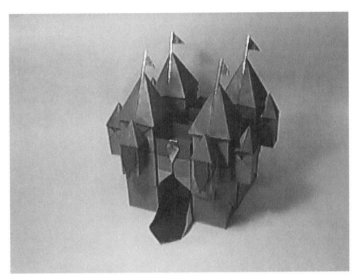

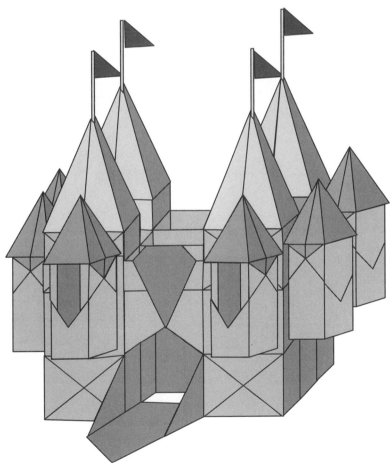

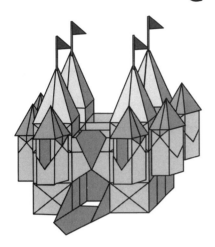

The first model in this book demonstrates how to create complex structures from just a few simple units. The process of using several units folded together to form a complex structure is called modular origami. The fairy tale castle is made up of 59 separate modules. Yet there are only 6 different types to fold. Since there are a great many complex structures to be found within the pages of this book, all of the models used in constructuion are to be found in the constructuion set section, at the beginning of the book.

Let's begin by looking at the photograph and drawing at the top of this page. You will see a castle that looks difficult to fold, but let me emphasize that the units used in the castle — building block, sleeve, roof, tower top, arched block, and a drawbridge — are simple to fold. The building block is made of two simple boxes that are folded together. The sleeve, which is a hollow cube , is used to hold the various unites together so that they will not unfold themselves over time. Origami models have a tendency to unfold as the paper relaxes. It is necessary to constrain the paper so that it cannot relax into an unrecognizable figure. The roof for the fairy tale castle is folded so that there are large flaps of paper that can be inserted into another unit to hold it in place. The tower top is a simple box with side flaps. The arched block forms an entrance to the castle, and holds the drawbridge. The drawbridge is an action model, a model that can be made to move. The drawbridge raises and lowers on the finished castle. Almost every unit in the fairy tale castle has flaps and pockets. The flaps are extended portions of paper that can be inserted into other units. Pockets are created in each unit to accomodate such flaps. This will seem complicated at first, but every step in the assembly of the castle is precisely documented.

Because of the size of the finished castle, you will undoubtedly want to take a break from folding at some point in its construction. This will not be a problem since the castle is made up of 4 towers, 3 walls, and 1 drawbridge assembly. These can be built individually, then assembled later. No glue is used in the construction of the castle. Glue is simply not permitted in origami.

Before you begin, let me suggest using a fairly stiff paper. Typing paper of almost any weight can be used. Butcher paper, which is available in craft stores, is another resource. Butcher paper comes in a wide variety of colors and was used in constructing the castle in the photograph. Construction paper can be used to make the castle, but it is very difficult to work with. When making your first castle, I suggest using a standard size of typing paper. This is easily available and also comes in bright colors. If you want to make the castle more in proportion to the other figures in the book, I suggest 10″ or 12″ squares of paper. It all depends on how much space you have. The castle can be dismantled and stored in a box or folded flat and stored in a large envelope.

When you have finished folding the fairy tale castle, you will need knights in shining armor, maidens fair, attendants, sorcerers, and of course, a king and queen.

The following units are needed to assemble the tower:
1 roof
1 half building block
1 sleeve
1 building block

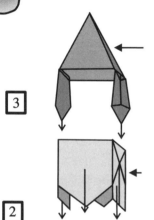

3

Roof
Attach the roof to the half building block by inserting its flaps into the sides of the half building block. Adjust the roof so that it overhangs on all four sides.

2

Half Building Block
Attach the half building block to the sleeve by inserting its flaps into the pockets of the sleeve.

Sleeve
Attach the sleeve to the building block by fitting it over the outside of the building block.

1

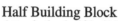 Building Block

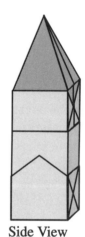

Side View   Front View

The drawings above show an exploded view of the castle tower and two views of the completed tower. I have given you two views so you can see the location of the pointed flaps. The flaps on the building blocks are used to connect the parts of the castle.

In step 1, you slip the sleeve over the complete building block. Be sure that the pockets inside the sleeve are at the top of the model when you do this. When you slide the sleeve over the building block, be careful to keep the pointed flaps of the building block on the outside of the sleeve. You can see one of these pointed flaps on the front view of the tower. The sleeve will slip all the way down to the bottom of the pointed flap.

In step 2, when you have the sleeve over the building block, insert all 4 flaps of the half building block into the pockets of the sleeve. There are 3 pockets inside the sleeve to receive these flaps. The remaining flap fits inside the sleeve.

In step 3, slip the pointed flaps of the roof into the side pockets of the half building block. Slide these flaps all the way down, until only the edges of the roof extend over the half building block. If you make the roof of the tower out of a bright color paper, you will enhance the appearance of your castle.

The following units are needed to assemble the wall:
- 1 tower top
- 1 sleeve
- 1 building block

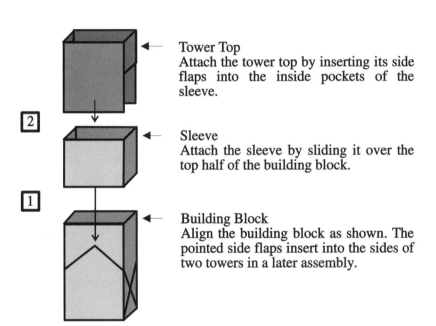

2

Tower Top
Attach the tower top by inserting its side flaps into the inside pockets of the sleeve.

Sleeve
Attach the sleeve by sliding it over the top half of the building block.

1

Building Block
Align the building block as shown. The pointed side flaps insert into the sides of two towers in a later assembly.

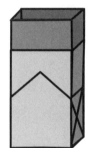

The drawings above show an exploded view of the castle wall and a completed wall.

In step 1, you slip the sleeve over a building block in the same way as in the construction of the tower. Be careful to keep the pointed flaps of the building block on the outside of the sleeve. These flaps are used in attaching the wall to the towers of the castle. When you place the sleeve over the building block, be sure that the pockets are on the top of the model.

In step 2, slide the flaps of the tower top into two of the pockets inside the sleeve. If you make the tower top out of the same bright colored paper as the roof, the appearance of your castle will be greatly enhanced.

You will need to make a total of 3 walls to complete the castle.

Drawbridge Assembly

The following units are needed to assemble the drawbridge:
- 1 tower top
- 1 arched block
- 1 drawbridge

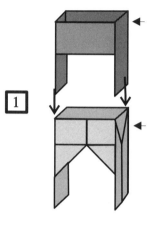

[1]

Tower Top
Attach the tower top by inserting its flaps into the sides of the arched block.

Arched Block
Attach the arched block to the building blocks of the two front towers during a later assembly.

Gatehouse

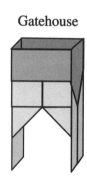

[2]

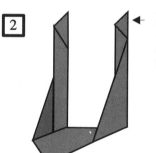

Drawbridge
Attach the drawbridge to the fairy tale castle during the last steps of the front assembly.

Drawbridge

The drawings above show a gatehouse and a drawbridge. In step 1, you can see how to insert the tower top flaps into the pockets in the sides of an arched block. These two models form the gatehouse, which will be used to hold the front of the castle together and to house the drawbridge. Step 2 shows a completed drawbridge. It will be placed in the gatehouse during the front assembly of the castle. The drawbridge can be made of brown paper to resemble wood, or black paper to resemble iron.

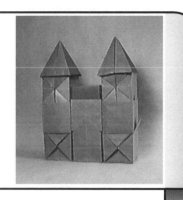

The following units are needed to assemble the back of the castle:
    2 tower assemblies
    1 wall assembly

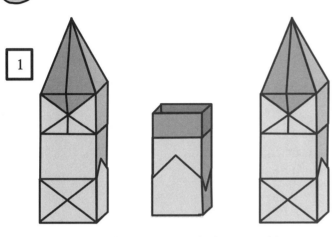

The back of the castle ready for assembly.

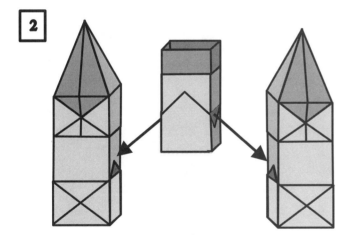

The pointed flaps on the sides of the wall
insert behind the pointed flaps on the towers.

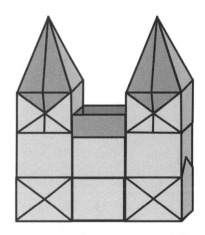

The back of the castle assembled.

   Arrange the 2 towers and the wall as shown in step 1, which is the view you would see if you were looking from the front of the castle. Note that the roof has the creases of the folds facing toward you, the wall has the building block model with the pointed flap facing up.

   In step 2, you can see how to insert the pointed flaps on the wall into the pointed flaps of the towers. These flaps have been shaded in the drawing to help you locate them. The back assembly is fairly easy since the wall is simply pushed down into the two towers.

The following units are needed to assemble the sides of the castle:
- 1 back assembly
- 2 tower assemblies
- 2 wall assemblies

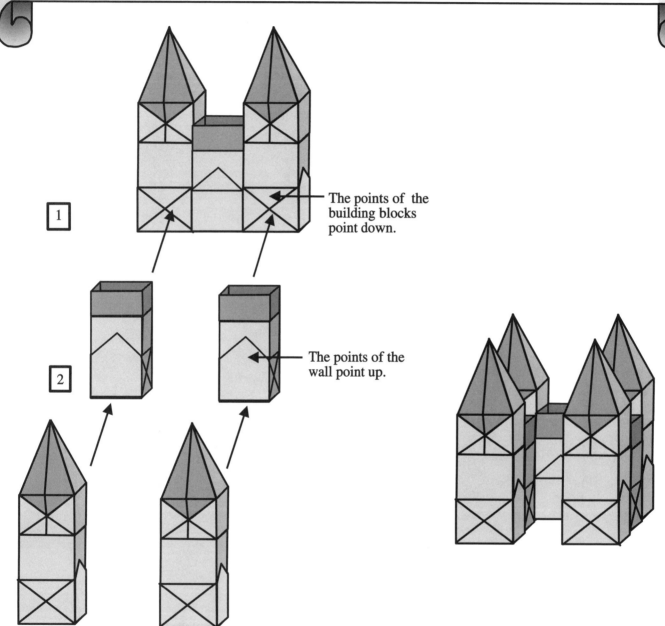

1

The points of the building blocks point down.

2

The points of the wall point up.

You will need the two remaining towers and walls to complete the side assembly. Arrange the back assembly and walls as they appear in steps 1 and 2. Notice the walls have the pointed flaps facing you, pointing up. This alignment will allow you to insert the building block flaps into the flaps on the back towers. This procedure is identical to the back assembly except the walls are pushed up into the tower flaps. Now assemble the front towers by pushing their flaps down into the pointed flaps of the walls.

The following units are needed to assemble the front of the castle:
   1 side assembly
   1 drawbridge assembly

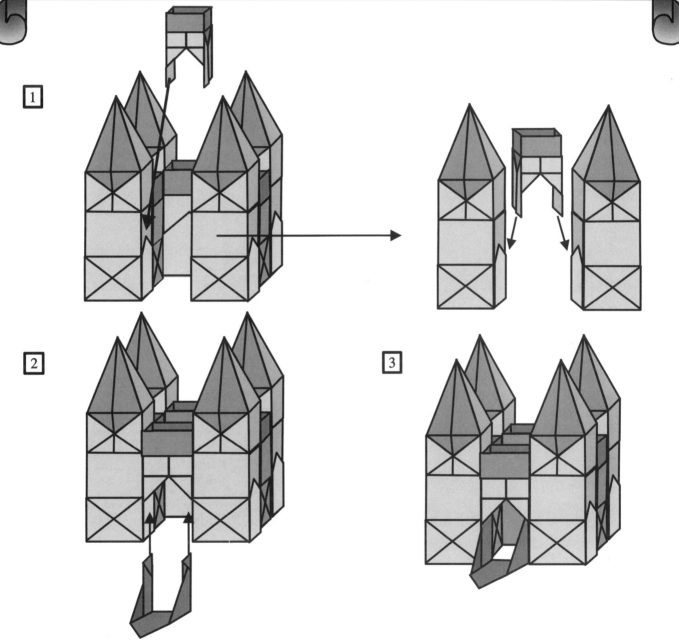

1

2

3

Step 1 shows how to attach the gatehouse. Simply push it all the way down into the side flaps of the two front towers so that the top of the arched block is even with the top of the sleeve. Take your time and be patient as you do this assembly. You will need to make sure that both flaps of the gatehouse are inside the tower flaps before you push it into position. Steps 2 and 3 show the drawbridge. Simply insert it into the gatehouse. Be sure that the side flaps extend fully inside the arched block of the gatehouse.

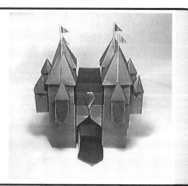

The following units are needed to assemble the turrets of the castle:
    8 turret assemblies

1

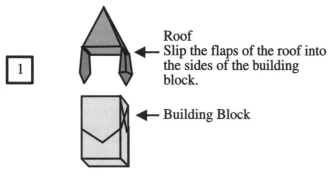

Roof
Slip the flaps of the roof into the sides of the building block.

Building Block

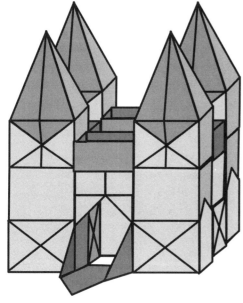

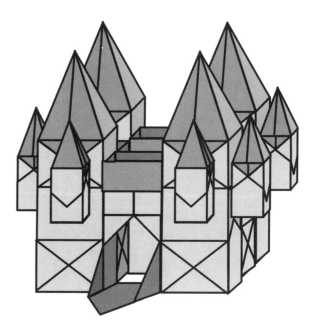

Eight side turrets are needed to complete the fairy tale castle. These turrets consist of a complete building block and a roof made from paper ¼ the size of that used for the other castle units. Step 1 shows how to assemble the turret. Simply push the side flaps of the roof down into the building block in the same way you assembled the castle towers. When you complete the turrets, you can hang them from the sides of the castle towers. Insert a pointed flap of a turret onto the sleeve of a tower. Two turrets should be assembled onto each tower. Try making the small turret roofs from the same colored paper as the tower roofs.

A Knight In Shining Armor

Knight Base

Fold the knight base from a 4″ square sheet of paper.

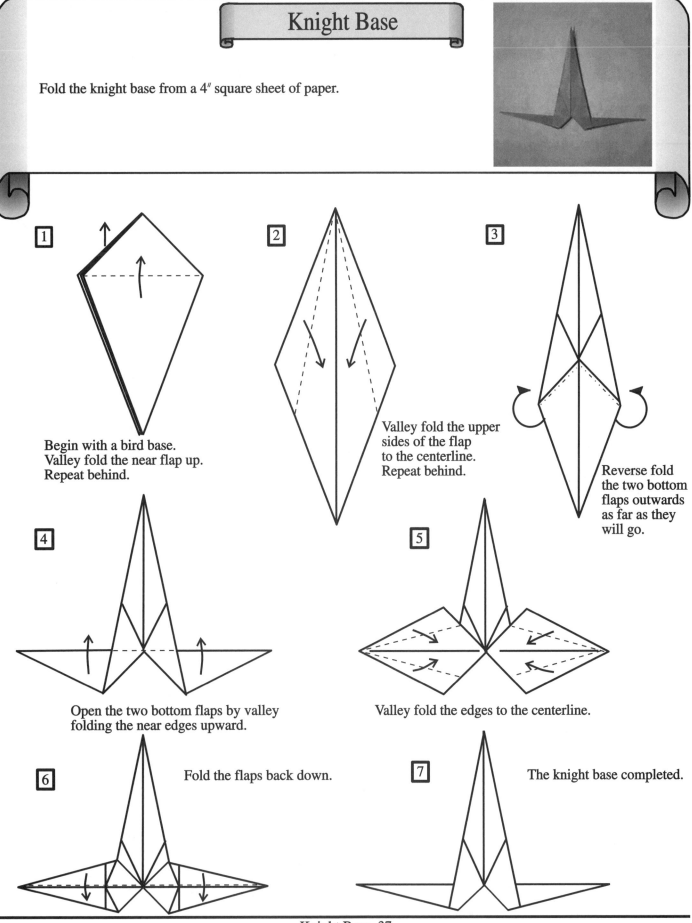

1

Begin with a bird base.
Valley fold the near flap up.
Repeat behind.

2

Valley fold the upper
sides of the flap
to the centerline.
Repeat behind.

3

Reverse fold
the two bottom
flaps outwards
as far as they
will go.

4

Open the two bottom flaps by valley
folding the near edges upward.

5

Valley fold the edges to the centerline.

Fold the flaps back down.

6

7

The knight base completed.

Knight

Fold the knight from two knight bases made from 4″ square sheets of paper.
Use foil-backed sheets of paper to make a knight in shining armor.
Candy wrappers provide an excellent source of paper.

Upper Half

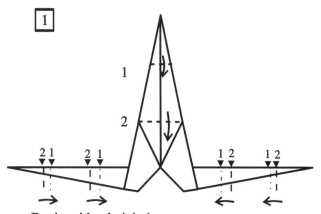

1

Begin with a knight base.
Valley fold the top flap down twice as shown.
Form the elbows and wrists by making in
order the reverse folds indicated.

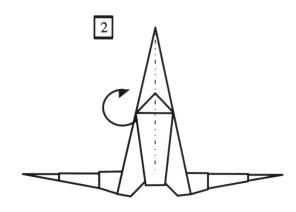

2

Mountain fold the paper in half.

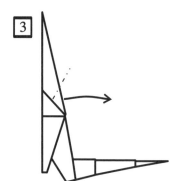

3

Inside reverse fold the
top point.

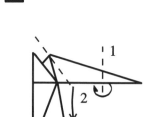

4

1 Outside reverse fold the end of the flap.
2 Outside reverse fold the flap to
form the head and face of the knight.

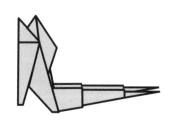

5

The completed upper
half of the knight.

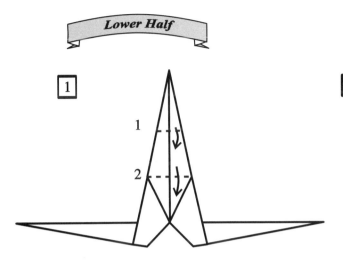
1

Begin with a knight base.
Valley fold the top flap down twice
as shown in the above drawing.

2

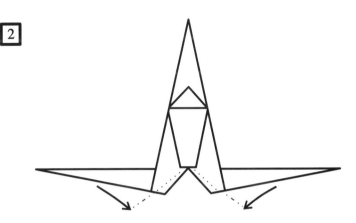

Reverse fold down the two side flaps. You will need to
fold in the small inner portion of these flaps as you
complete these folds. These folds are necessary to form
the hips of the knight. You can increase the angle of the
upper part of the legs by adjusting the amount of reverse
fold. If you decrease the angle of these folds, the model
of the knight can be made to bow.

3

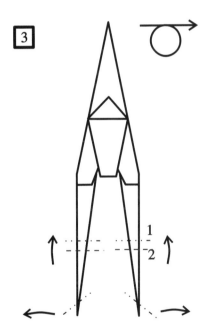

Form the knight's knees by making in
order the reverse folds indicated.
Reverse fold the bottoms of these flaps
to form the feet.
Turn the model over.

4

Valley fold the model in
half along the centerline.

5

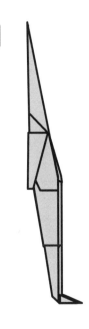

Lower half of the knight
ready for assembly.

1 Open the upper and lower halves of the knight.
Insert the back pointed flap of the lower half into the back of the upper half.

2 Fold the back flaps of the upper half back down to fix in place the flap of the lower half.
Mountain fold the entire figure along the centerline.

3 A knight in shining armor ready to articulate.

The drawings above show how to assemble the two units used to form the knight. You will need to unfold the upper half of the knight, back to the knight base, before you can fold the two models together. Since the paper has already been folded once, it will be much easier to refold.

Arrange the models as you see them in step 1. First open up the two flaps of the upper model enough to insert the top flap of the lower model inside. The front flap of the lower model is inserted into the upper model. You can adjust the height of your knight by adjusting the amount of flap you insert into the upper unit. Step 2 shows you where to position the flap of the lower unit to make a knight of average height.

Refold the back flap of the upper half along its original creases. This will lock the upper and lower halves of the knight together. Mountain fold the whole model along the centerline. Refold the head of the knight as you did when you made the upper half. Step 3 shows the knight ready for articulation.

Sword

Fold the knight's sword from a 2″ square sheet of paper. Foil-backed paper such as a candy wrapper, gives your knight's sword a metallic shine.

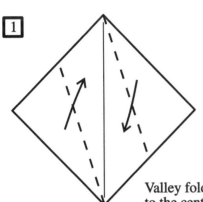

1

Valley fold the sides to the centerline.

2

Valley fold the sides to the centerline.

3

Valley fold the sides to the centerline.

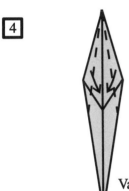

4

Valley fold the sides to the centerline.

5

Valley fold the sides to the centerline.

6

Valley fold the model in half along the centerline.

Assembly Instructions

Unfold the back of the knight. Insert the sword under the top flap of the lower half of the knight until the bottom of the sword is even with the feet of the knight. Refold the knight with the sword in place. This simple sword will allow the knight to stand up.

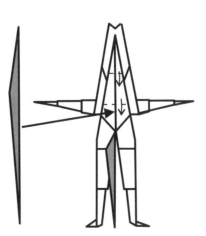

Shield

Fold the knight's shield from a 2″ square sheet of paper.

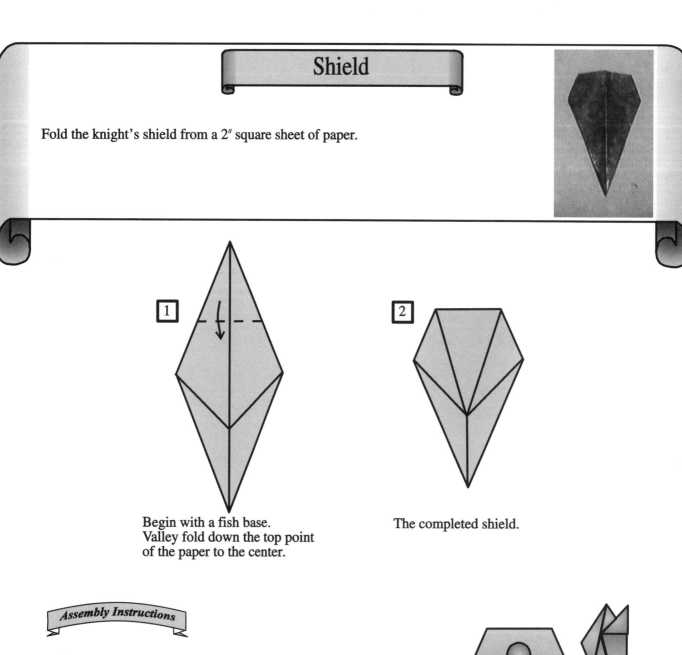

1

Begin with a fish base.
Valley fold down the top point
of the paper to the center.

2

The completed shield.

Assembly Instructions

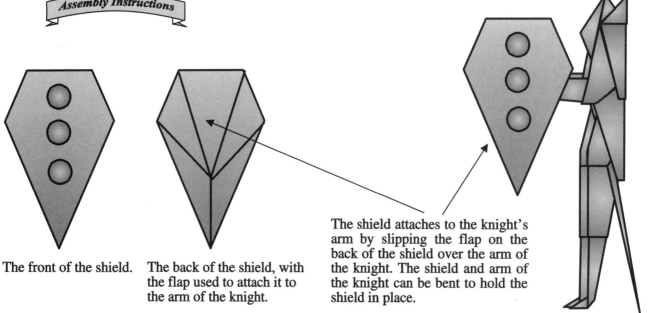

The front of the shield.

The back of the shield, with
the flap used to attach it to
the arm of the knight.

The shield attaches to the knight's
arm by slipping the flap on the
back of the shield over the arm of
the knight. The shield and arm of
the knight can be bent to hold the
shield in place.

Lance & Standard

Fold the knight's lance from a 6″ x 1″ rectangular sheet of paper.
Fold the knight's standard from a 1″ square sheet of paper.

Lance

1 Roll the paper about halfway around a toothpick.

2 Slide the toothpick out of the paper.

3 Continue to roll the paper until it is very tight.

4 You can make a point on the lance
by pushing out the center of the paper.
A completed lance for the knight.

Standard

1

Fold the small square of paper in half
along both diagonals and unfold.

Unroll the lance far enough to insert the square
of paper. The paper should extend out from the
lance about halfway. Roll up the lance with the
standard at the end. Standards can also be flown
from the castles.

2

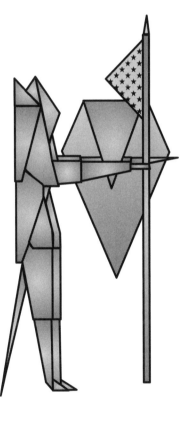

The Knight's Hands

The hands of the human characters in the book can be folded to hold any small object without the use of glue. These folds work best with a foil-backed paper.

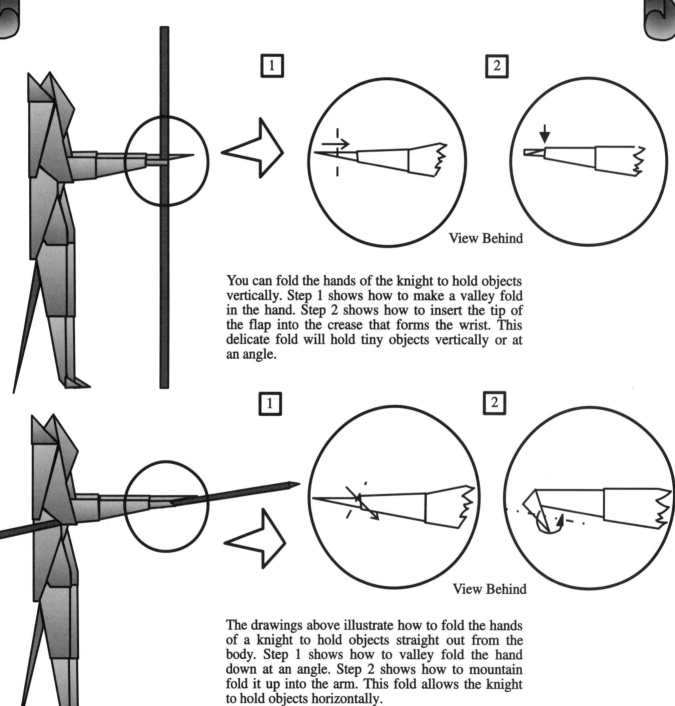

View Behind

You can fold the hands of the knight to hold objects vertically. Step 1 shows how to make a valley fold in the hand. Step 2 shows how to insert the tip of the flap into the crease that forms the wrist. This delicate fold will hold tiny objects vertically or at an angle.

View Behind

The drawings above illustrate how to fold the hands of a knight to hold objects straight out from the body. Step 1 shows how to valley fold the hand down at an angle. Step 2 shows how to mountain fold it up into the arm. This fold allows the knight to hold objects horizontally.

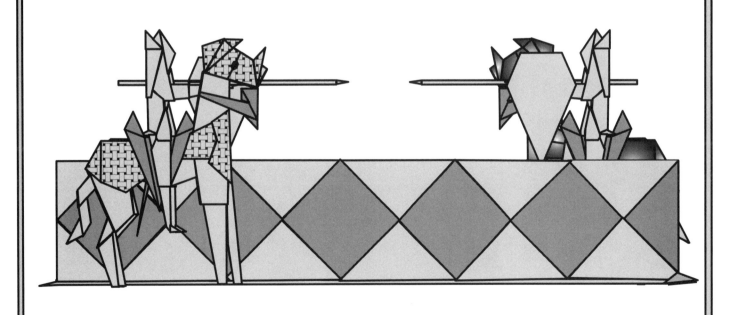

Horse

Fold the knight's horse from two 6″ square sheets of paper.

Rear Half

1

Begin with a bird base.
Valley fold the near flap up.
Repeat behind.

2

Valley fold the sides
to the centerline.
Repeat behind.

3

Valley fold the top
flap and unfold.
Open up the side flaps.

4

Form an off-center rabbit ear
of the top flap at the intersection
of the lines formed in step 3.

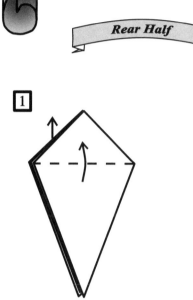

5

Working from the right,
narrow the sharp flap with
valley folds on both
of its sides.

◄ In Progress ►

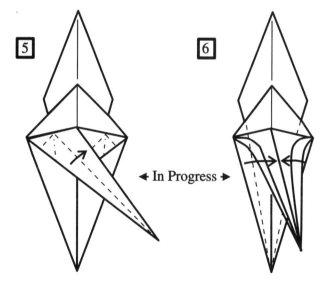

6

Fold the left and right
edges to the centerline
along existing creases.

7

The center flap becomes
the horse's tail.

8

Mountain fold in half.
Rotate it to the position
shown in step 9.

Horse 47

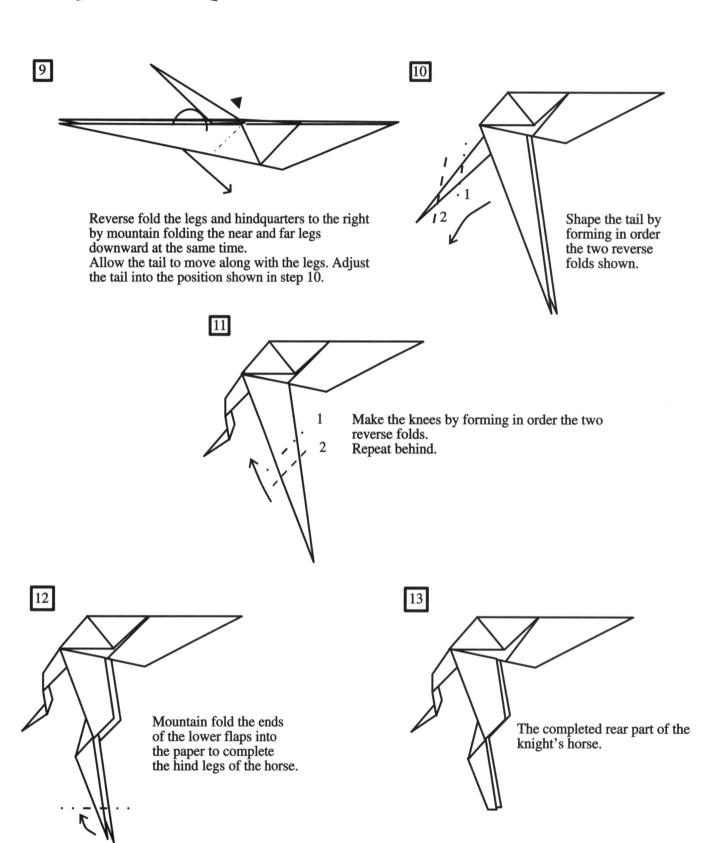

9

Reverse fold the legs and hindquarters to the right by mountain folding the near and far legs downward at the same time.
Allow the tail to move along with the legs. Adjust the tail into the position shown in step 10.

10

Shape the tail by forming in order the two reverse folds shown.

11

1   Make the knees by forming in order the two
2   reverse folds.
    Repeat behind.

12

Mountain fold the ends of the lower flaps into the paper to complete the hind legs of the horse.

13

The completed rear part of the knight's horse.

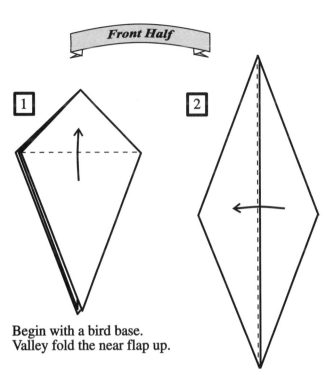

1

Begin with a bird base.
Valley fold the near flap up.

2

Valley fold the
near right flap
to the left.

3

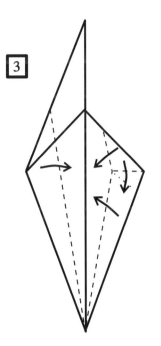

Valley fold the left long side
to the centerline.
Working from the bottom
with a single flap, form a
rabbit ear at the right; flatten
leftward the right corner as
shown.

4

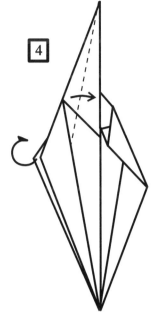

Valley fold the near left
flap to the centerline.
Swing the far left flap
to the right.
Then repeat steps 3–4
behind.

5

Open the paper
to look like this.
Mountain fold
the paper in half
along centerline.

6

Outside reverse fold
the top flap down.
Reverse fold the
center flap up.

7

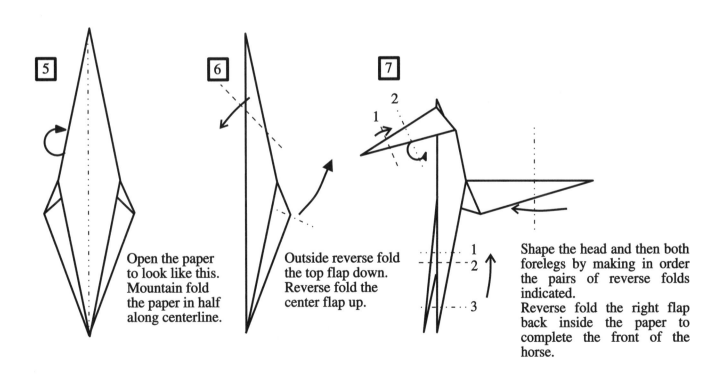

Shape the head and then both
forelegs by making in order
the pairs of reverse folds
indicated.
Reverse fold the right flap
back inside the paper to
complete the front of the
horse.

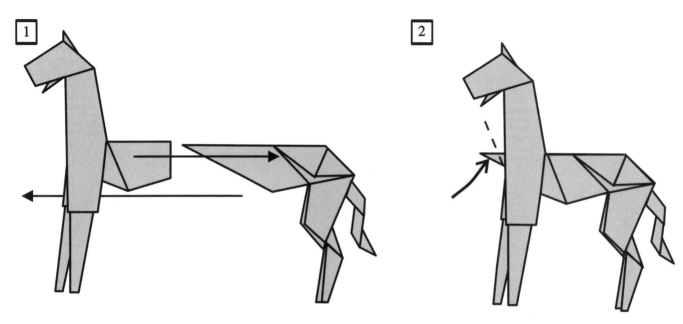

1

Slide the rear model through the legs of the front half. Insert the flap on the front half under the flap on the back of the rear half.

2

Outside reverse fold the flap that extends under the head of the horse. This will lock the two halves together without the use of glue.

The drawings above show how to assemble the knight's horse. You may have to adjust several of the flaps on the front and rear halves of the horse. If you do not have enough flap extending in front of the horse to lock the front and rear halves together, you will have to shorten the flap that extends into the back of the horse. Adjust the feet of the horse so that the assembled model will stand up by itself. Each of the legs can be adjusted to make the horse appear to be standing or running while in a joust. The flap on the back of the horse is very important. This flap will lock the saddle and the knight onto the horse without the need for glue. There are also pockets on the horse for attaching the armor (caparisons), as well as the saddle and bridle.

Jousting Bridle

Fold the jousting bridle from a 2″ square sheet of paper.

1

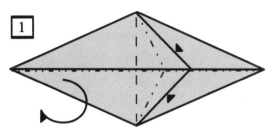

Begin with a fish base.
Squash fold the two center flaps.
Mountain fold the paper in half along the centerline.

2

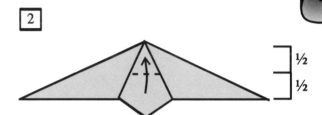

½
½

Valley fold the near central flap upward to a point beyond the top, so that it will touch the top edges at its widest points.

3

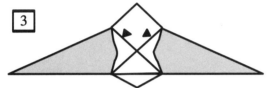

Flatten the inner edges outward, squashing them into the position shown in step 4.

4

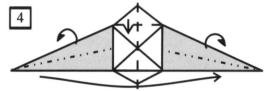

Valley fold the small flap at the top to the center. Mountain fold all the paper except the very top layer as you valley fold the paper in half.

5

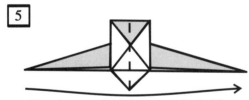

Continue to fold the paper in half.

6

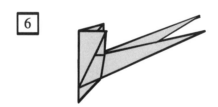

The completed jousting bridle.

Assembly Instructions

Fold down the flap under the chin of the horse. Insert this flap into the folds of the bridle.

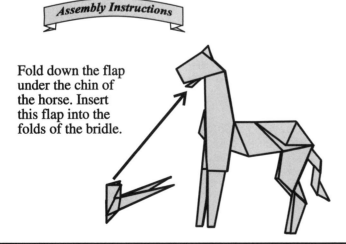

Mountain fold the side flaps into the neck of the horse. When you fold the side flaps back they pinch the bridle onto the lower jaw of the horse.

Jousting Saddle

Fold the jousting saddle from a 2″ square sheet of paper.

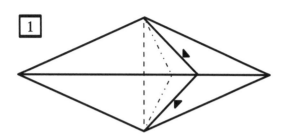

1

Begin with a white fish base.
Squash fold the two center flaps.

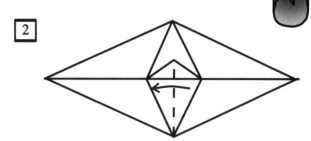

2

Valley fold the lower center flap.

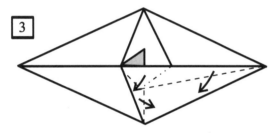

3

Working from the right, form the near lower layer into a
rabbit ear. Open the center flap as you accomplish this fold.
Repeat steps 2–3 on the left side of the model.

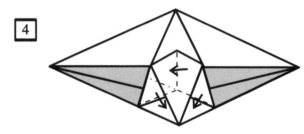

4

Your paper should look like this.
Fold the central flap into a rabbit ear.

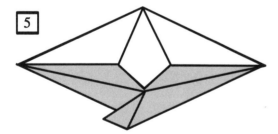

5

Repeat steps 2–4 on the opposite
side.

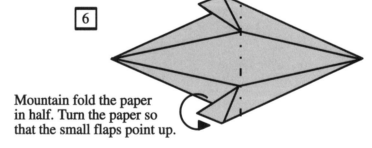

6

Mountain fold the paper
in half. Turn the paper so
that the small flaps point up.

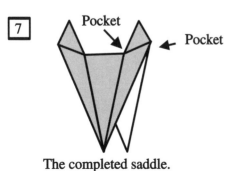

7

Pocket

Pocket

The completed saddle.

Assembly Instructions

Attach the saddle to the
horse by inserting the
flap on the back of the
horse into the pocket on
the back of the saddle.

The Mounted Knight

The following units are needed to assemble the mounted knight:
- 1 knight
- 1 shield
- 1 lance
- 1 horse
- 1 jousting saddle
- 1 jousting bridle

The lance fits under the right arm and crosses over to the left side of the horse.

The shield slips over the left arm of the knight. You may want to bend the shield and the arm of the knight to secure it in place.

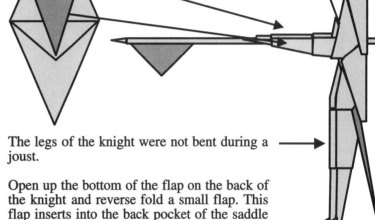

The legs of the knight were not bent during a joust.

Open up the bottom of the flap on the back of the knight and reverse fold a small flap. This flap inserts into the back pocket of the saddle to hold the knight on the horse.

The shield and the lance both were held on the left side of the horse during a joust. Flags were removed from the lance prior to a joust.

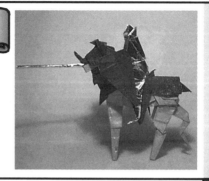

The well-armored medieval horse wore the shaffron to protect its nose, the peytral to protect its front, and the cruppers to protect its back, which are each folded from a 2″ square sheet of paper. Use foil-backed paper to make the caparisons resemble metal armor, a colorful patterned paper to resemble a quilted fabric, or a mottled brown paper to resemble leather. As a rule, the metal armor was very heavy and worn only by the wealthiest of men.

Paper that looks like metal.

Paper that looks like quilted fabric.

Paper that looks like leather.

Squires and attendants often had the horses dressed with the colors of their knights when they attended a jousting tournament.

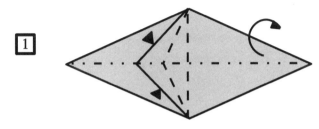

1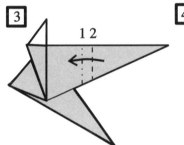

Begin with a fish base.
Squash fold the small flaps down on both sides.
Mountain fold the model in half along centerline.

2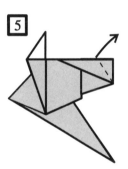

Valley fold the small flap on the centerline.
Repeat behind.
Reverse fold the left side of the model.

3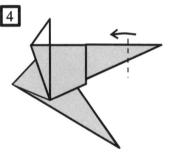

Form in order the two
reverse folds shown.

4

Outside reverse fold the end
of the right flap.

5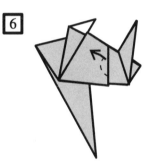

Outside reverse fold
the end of the flap up.

6

Open up the eye folds.

Assembly Instructions

Attach the shaffron to the
horse by slipping its flap
into the neck of the
horse. The headpiece of
the shaffron slips over
the head of the horse.

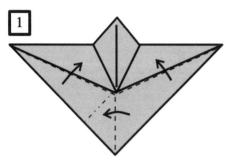

Begin with step 2 of the jousting bridle. Unfold the bottom half and form it into a rabbit ear.

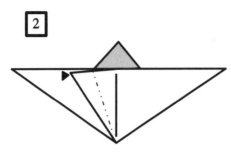

Squash fold the center flap.

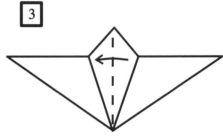

Valley fold the center flap in half.

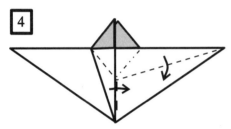

Working from the right, fold the near layer downward in half; a collar will form itself at the left. Repeat with the left half of the model.

Pinch the center flap into a kind of rabbit ear and flatten it to the left.

Lift and squash the small central flap.

Mountain fold the paper in half along the centerline.

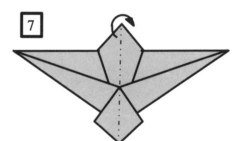

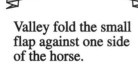
Valley fold the small flap against one side of the horse.

Place the Peytral on the front of the horse and fold the side flaps into the legs of the horse.

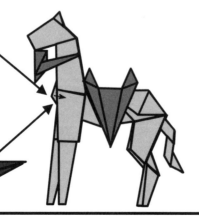

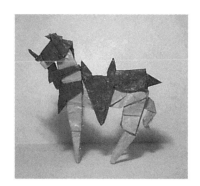

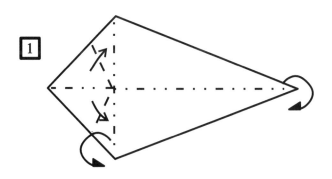

1

Begin with a kite base.
Mountain and valley fold the left side of the flap as you mountain fold the paper in half along the centerline.

2

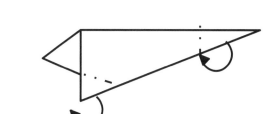

Reverse fold the right end.
Mountain fold the lower point up into the model.
Repeat behind.

3

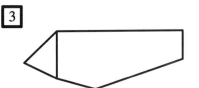

The completed cruppers, ready for assembly onto the horse.

Assembly Instructions

Attach the cruppers to the hind quarters of the knight's horse by slipping the front part between the two flaps of the saddle. You can fasten the model onto the horse more securely by first removing the saddle. Unfold the small flap on the front of the cruppers and fold it under the flap on the back of the horse. Replace the saddle under the cruppers flap.

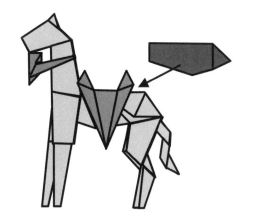

1 2 3 4 5

6

Pockets

Flaps

Pockets

Flap

The drawings above show how models can be folded into almost any pose by reverse-folding the flaps. Reverse folds can be used at joints when the model needs to sit or have an arm or leg bent. When a reverse fold is applied to a model, the pleat folds occur at the same place as the original model, but their direction may be reversed. Experiment with the models to find the best way to utilize the reverse folds. Drawing 6 shows some of the pockets and flaps that can be used to fold in other models.

Knight's Attendants

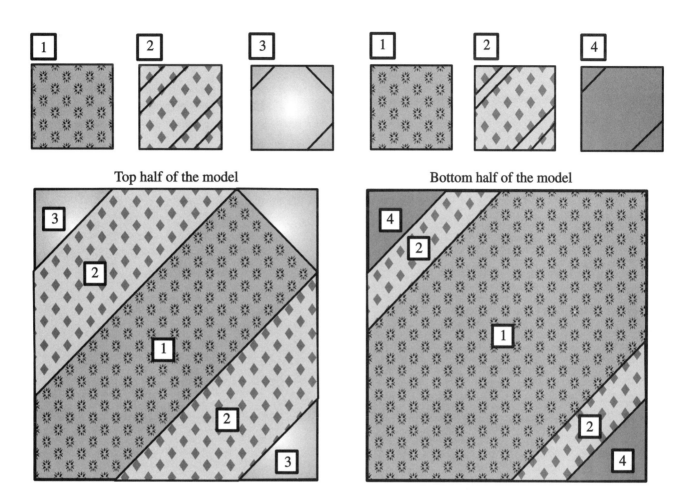

Top half of the model

Bottom half of the model

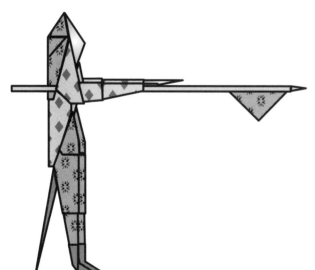

A knight's attendant made from the papers described above.

The knight's attendants were the pages and squires. These young men and boys were responsible for taking care of the knight's belongings. They attended to the knight's horse and all the weapons he needed for a joust or during a battle. They often wore clothes containing the colors and emblems of the knight they served. By making your own paper, you can achieve an attendant with the colors of a knight you have folded. Drawing 1 shows the primary sheet of paper. Drawing 2 shows a second color and where to cut the paper to glue onto the primary sheet. Drawings 3 and 4 show the flesh-colored paper and a paper of black or brown for the attendant's boots. Imagination is the key in making your attendants.

Flags and pennants can be made of the colors you choose for your knight. The maidens who attended the jousts might have been daughters of these knights and they too would have worn their fathers' colors. Their blouses and skirts can be made of the same paper as the attendants.

Maiden Fair

Fold the maiden fair by making a knight base and an eight-sided cone, each out of a 4″ square sheet of paper. The maiden's hat is another eight-sided cone made from a 1½″ square sheet of paper

1

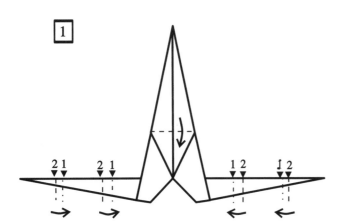

Begin with a knight base.
Valley fold the top flap down as shown.
Then form the elbows and wrists by making in order the pairs of reverse folds indicated.

2

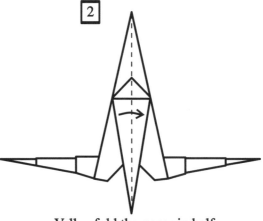

Valley fold the paper in half along the centerline.

3

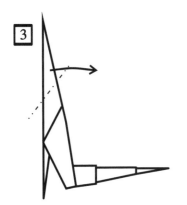

Inside reverse fold the top point of paper.

4

Outside reverse fold the end of the flap.
Outside reverse fold the flap of paper to form the head and face of the maiden.

5

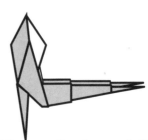

The completed upper half of the maiden.

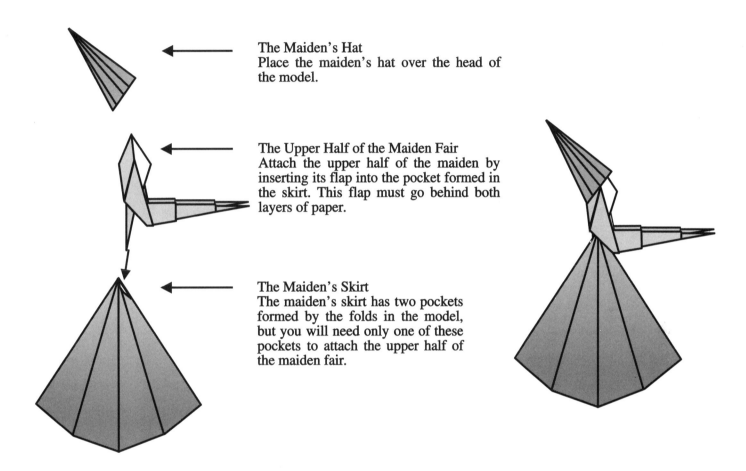

The Maiden's Hat
Place the maiden's hat over the head of the model.

The Upper Half of the Maiden Fair
Attach the upper half of the maiden by inserting its flap into the pocket formed in the skirt. This flap must go behind both layers of paper.

The Maiden's Skirt
The maiden's skirt has two pockets formed by the folds in the model, but you will need only one of these pockets to attach the upper half of the maiden fair.

The above drawings show an exploded view of the maiden fair and a completed model. Use a toothpick to open up one of the folds in the eight-sided cone, and insert the flap of the upper half of the maiden fair. It is important to insert the flap under both folds of paper in the cone. The eight-sided cone will open slightly as you insert the flap. Slide the upper half of the maiden fair down into the cone until only the maiden's face can be seen. After you are satisfied with this portion of the assembly, try to fold the upper half of the maiden along the centerline. This will help hold it in place and improve the appearance of the model.

Open up the hat and place it over the head of the maiden fair. When the hat is in place, squeeze the head of the maiden along the centerline fold and the hat will remain in place.

The Campaign Tent

Fold the campaign tent from two 8″ square sheets of paper.

Lower Half

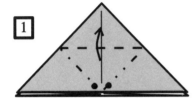

Start with a waterbomb base.
Lift the near lower edge all the way to the top,
squashing the side flaps into the position shown
in step 2.
Watch the black dots.
This is the same procedure as the building block.

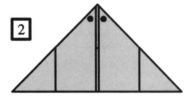

Your paper should look like this.
Repeat step 1 behind.

Valley fold the near single
layers to the upper edges.

Valley fold the paper in half
along the centerline.
Repeat behind.

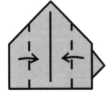

Valley fold the sides to the centerline.
Repeat behind.

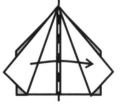

Open up the tent and
crease the edges of its top.

1

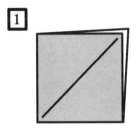

Begin with step 4 of the roof model.
Turn the model to look like step 2.

2

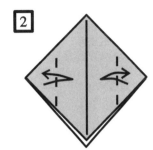

Valley fold the sides to the center.
Unfold these folds.

3

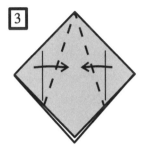

Valley fold the sides toward the
center from the top point to the
crease mark made in step 2.

4

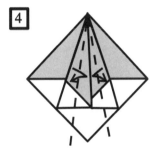

Valley fold toward the center the near
left flap, folding it exactly in half.
Unfold. Repeat on the right.

5

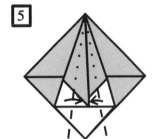

Valley fold the sides inside the
vertical pockets, rolling the
sides in toward the center.

6

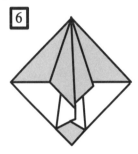

Your paper should look like this.
Repeat steps 2–5 behind.

7

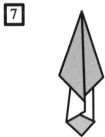

Open the paper up and crease
the folds.

8

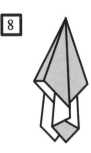

The completed upper half
of the campaign tent.

← The Upper Half of the Campaign Tent
Attach the upper half of the campaign tent by inserting its bottom flaps into the sides of the lower half. The upper half should fit inside the points of the lower half.

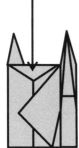

← The Lower Half of the Campaign Tent
The lower half of the campaign tent has flaps folded on its sides to hold the upper half of the campaign tent. You may wish to open these flaps slightly.

Side View

Front View

1

A completed tent open on only one side.

2

A campaign tent closed on both sides. Folded without folding steps 3–4 of the lower half.

3

A campaign tent open on both sides. Repeat step 3 of the lower half on both sides.

Joust Barricade

Fold the joust barricade from two 8″ square sheets of paper.

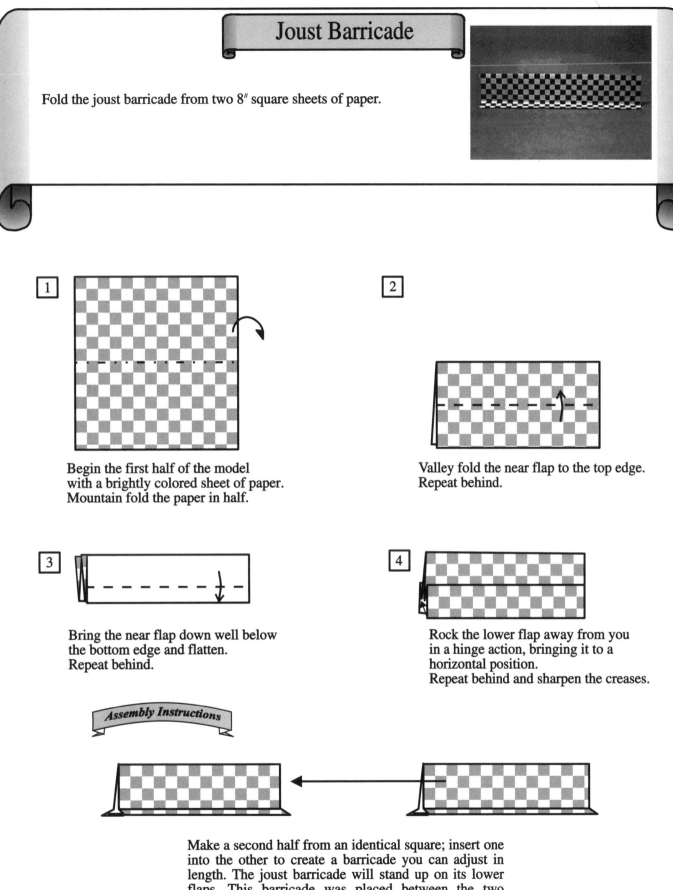

1

Begin the first half of the model with a brightly colored sheet of paper. Mountain fold the paper in half.

2

Valley fold the near flap to the top edge. Repeat behind.

3

Bring the near flap down well below the bottom edge and flatten. Repeat behind.

4

Rock the lower flap away from you in a hinge action, bringing it to a horizontal position. Repeat behind and sharpen the creases.

Assembly Instructions

Make a second half from an identical square; insert one into the other to create a barricade you can adjust in length. The joust barricade will stand up on its lower flaps. This barricade was placed between the two jousting knights.

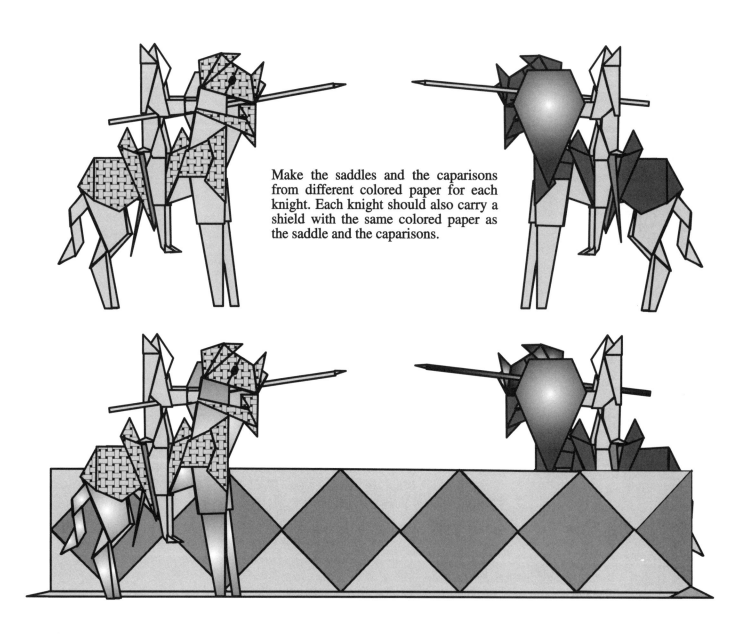

Make the saddles and the caparisons from different colored paper for each knight. Each knight should also carry a shield with the same colored paper as the saddle and the caparisons.

The drawings above show how to set up a joust. You will need two mounted knights and a barricade. You can use horses with or without the caparisons. Remember that the knights always held their lances in their right hands. The lance crosses over the horse to the left side when in a joust. The shield is held on the left arm to protect the knight against his opponent. You may also want to have the campaign tents for each knight and as many attendants as you wish to fold.

Merlin's Domain

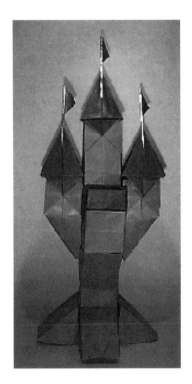

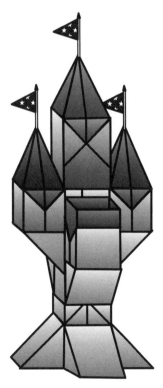

Merlin the Sorcerer

Fold Merlin by making a knight from two 4″ square sheets of the laminated paper described below, a knight's sword from a 2″ square sheet of paper, an eight-sided cone from a 1½″ square sheet of paper (his hat), and a lance from a 6″ x 1″ rectangular sheet of paper (his staff). You will need another 4″ square sheet of paper for Merlin's cloak.

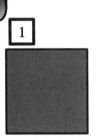 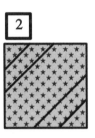 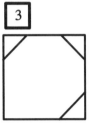 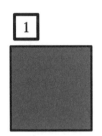 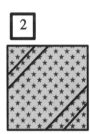 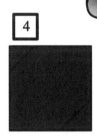

Top half of the model

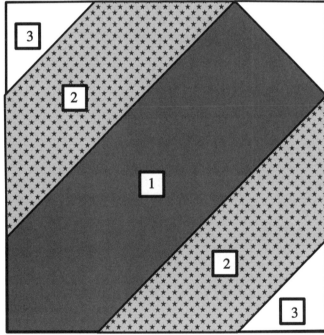

Bottom half of the model

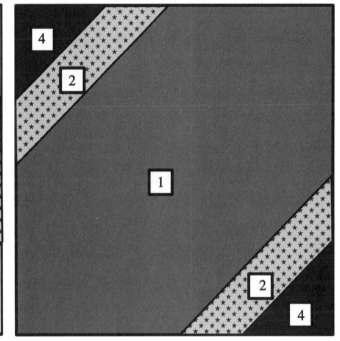

Merlin made from the papers described above.

Merlin appears in almost all of the Arthurian legends. He is folded like the knight and the attendants. The drawings above show how to make paper that will add to Merlin's appearance. Drawing 1 shows the primary sheet of paper. Drawing 2 shows a second color and where to cut the paper to glue it onto the primary sheet. Drawings 3 and 4 show the flesh-colored paper and a paper of black or brown for Merlin's boots. Imagination is the key to making your models.

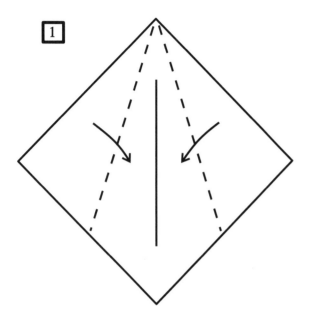

Valley fold the sides to the centerline.

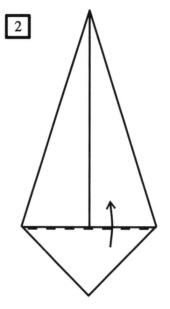

Valley fold the bottom flap up.

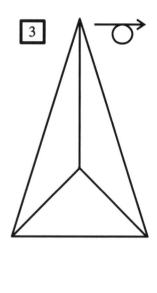

Turn the paper over.

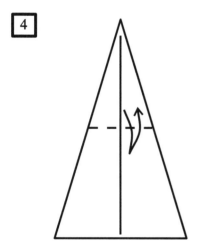

Find the center point by folding the top point down and making a small crease. Unfold.

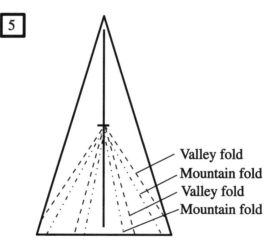

Valley fold
Mountain fold
Valley fold
Mountain fold

Pleat the bottom of the cloak.
The folds should run from the mark to the bottom of the paper.

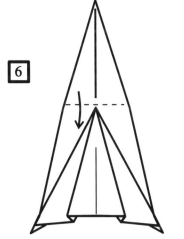

6 Valley fold down the top part of the paper just above the center point.

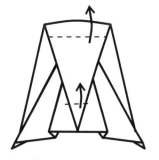

7 Valley fold up the small point of the top flap.
Valley fold up the entire flap.

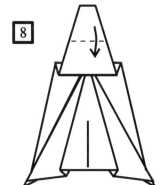

8 Valley fold in half downward.

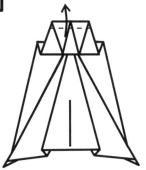

9 Valley fold the near flap up as indicated.

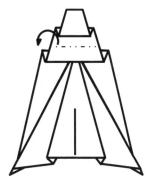

10 Mountain fold back the top flap.

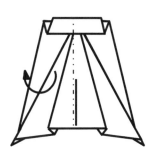

11 Mountain fold the paper in half.

12 Merlin's cloak completed.

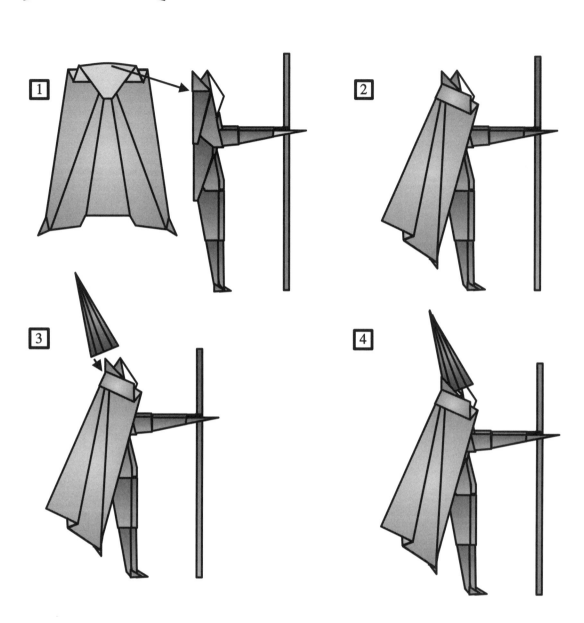

Merlin is assembled from several small units. You will need to fold the knight using a dark paper. Merlin's cloak can be folded from the same color paper or a contrasting color. The hat is the same used in folding the maiden fair. I suggest using black paper for the hat. The staff held by Merlin is a simple version of the lance.

Step 1 shows how to attach the cloak. You will need to open the model of Merlin enough to slip in the back flap of the cloak. Refold both models to hold the cloak in place. Step 2 shows the models together. Step 3 shows how to attach the hat. The hat is also held onto Merlin by the flap in the back of Merlin's head. The staff is held in Merlin's hand as the lance is held by the knight. Step 4 shows the completed Merlin.

Fold Vivian from two 4″ square sheets of paper and her belt and buckle from a 4″ x ½″ rectangular strip of paper.

Vivian's Skirt

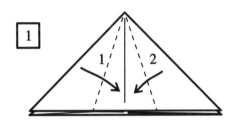

1

Start with a waterbomb base. Valley fold the top layer in thirds-the same folds as the eight-sided cone. Repeat behind.

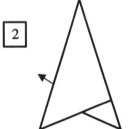

2

Pull out the internal flap at the left.

3

Valley fold the flap from step 2 under the near flap. Form a horizontal crease and unfold.

4

Mountain fold the tip of the left flap into the pocket formed by the lower edges of the right flap. Then valley fold the right flap upward into the pocket formed by the two nearest layers of the model.
Repeat behind.

5

Mountain fold the bottom flap into the pocket behind the flap. Repeat behind.

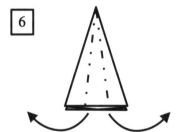

6

Open out the model and mountain fold each side in half.

7

A completed six-sided cone used as the skirt for Vivian.

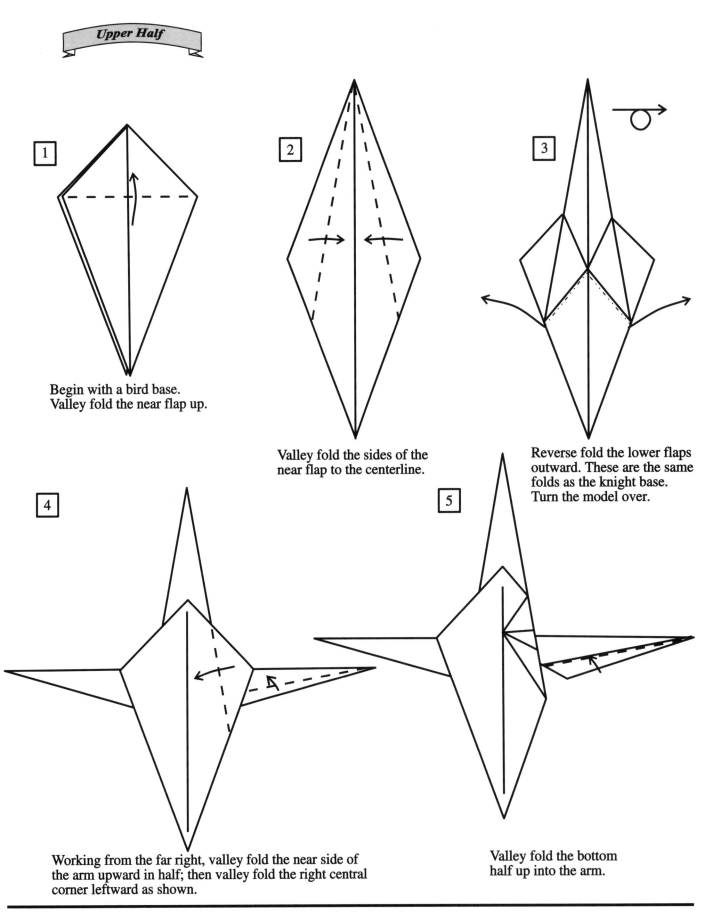

1

Begin with a bird base.
Valley fold the near flap up.

2

Valley fold the sides of the
near flap to the centerline.

3

Reverse fold the lower flaps
outward. These are the same
folds as the knight base.
Turn the model over.

4

Working from the far right, valley fold the near side of
the arm upward in half; then valley fold the right central
corner leftward as shown.

5

Valley fold the bottom
half up into the arm.

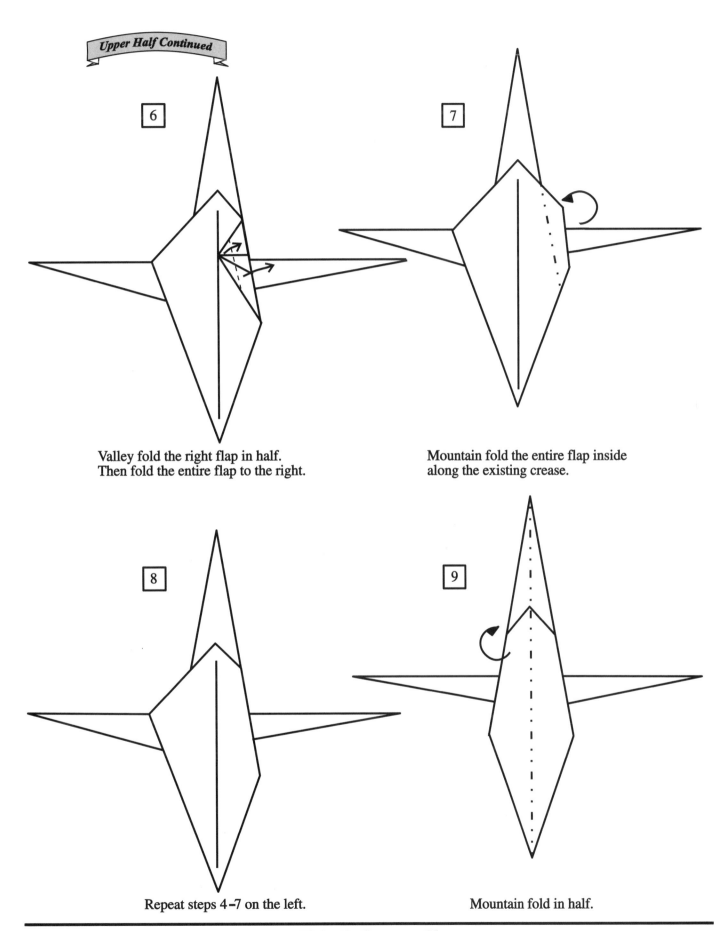

6

Valley fold the right flap in half.
Then fold the entire flap to the right.

7

Mountain fold the entire flap inside
along the existing crease.

8

Repeat steps 4–7 on the left.

9

Mountain fold in half.

10

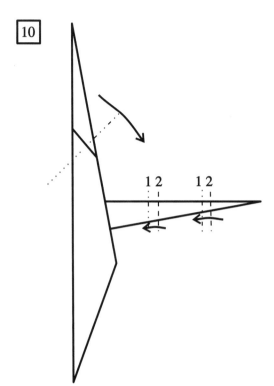

1 2   1 2

Inside reverse fold the top flap down.
Form the elbow and wrist by making
in order the reverse folds as shown.

11

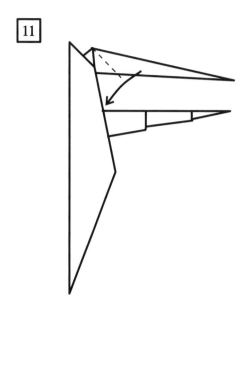

Outside reverse fold down the top right flap.
This flap is used to attach the upper half to
the skirt.

12

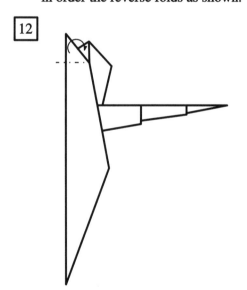

Reverse fold the small flap behind the
head straight down into the model.

13

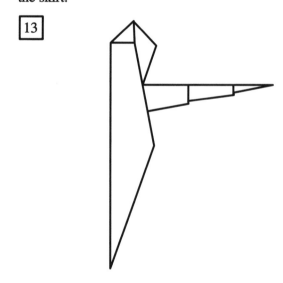

The complete upper half of Vivian.

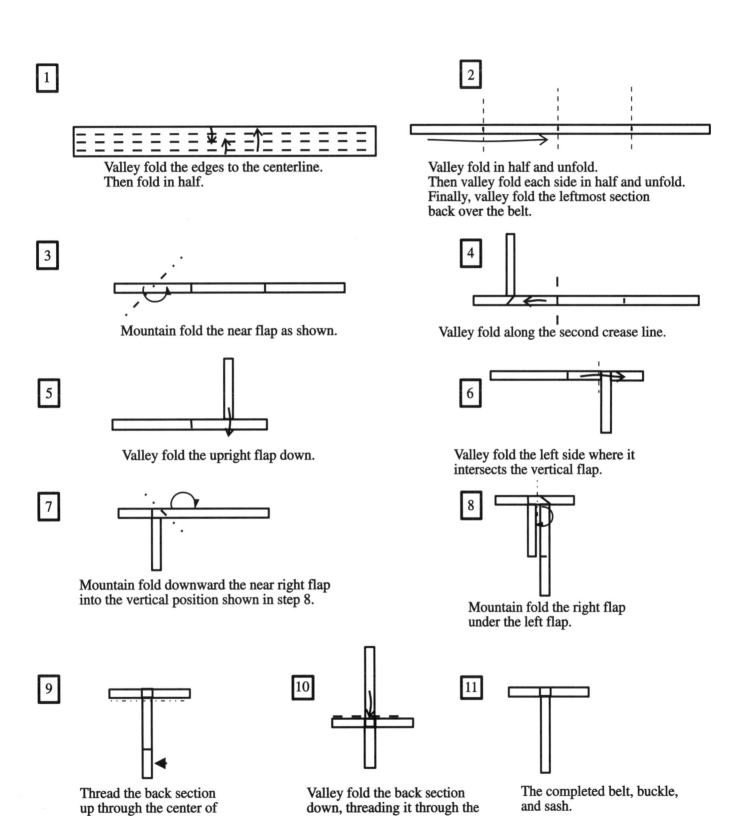

1

Valley fold the edges to the centerline.
Then fold in half.

2

Valley fold in half and unfold.
Then valley fold each side in half and unfold.
Finally, valley fold the leftmost section
back over the belt.

3

Mountain fold the near flap as shown.

4

Valley fold along the second crease line.

5

Valley fold the upright flap down.

6

Valley fold the left side where it
intersects the vertical flap.

7

Mountain fold downward the near right flap
into the vertical position shown in step 8.

8

Mountain fold the right flap
under the left flap.

9

Thread the back section
up through the center of
the belt.

10

Valley fold the back section
down, threading it through the
buckle on the front flap.

11

The completed belt, buckle,
and sash.

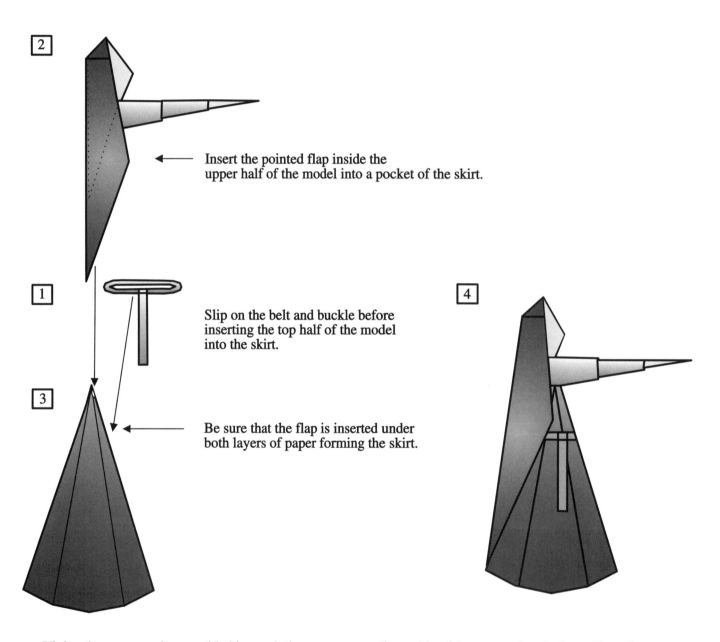

Insert the pointed flap inside the upper half of the model into a pocket of the skirt.

Slip on the belt and buckle before inserting the top half of the model into the skirt.

Be sure that the flap is inserted under both layers of paper forming the skirt.

Vivian the sorceress is assembled in much the same way as the maiden fair, except that the large flap of paper on the upper half of Vivian is not used in the assembly. Instead, the lower portion of Vivian's head, the narrow flap inside the upper unit, is inserted into the front of the six-sided cone. Before you can insert the flap, though, you must put the belt and buckle onto the six-sided cone. Adjust the belt and buckle to face the front of Vivian as shown in step 4.

Merlin's Dragon

Fold Merlin's dragon from three 6″ square sheets of paper, and his wings from one 6″ square sheet in a contrasting color.

Dragon's Head

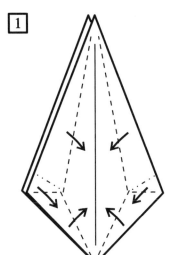

1

Begin with a bird base. Form the near right and left flaps into rabbit ears.

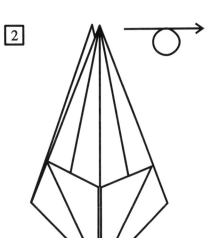

2

The paper should look like this. Turn the model over.

3

Fold the near flap into a configuration of a rabbit-ear type as shown.

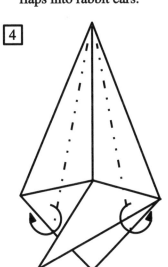

4

Mountain fold the near left flap in half, tucking it into the model. Repeat on the right.

5

Turn the model over.

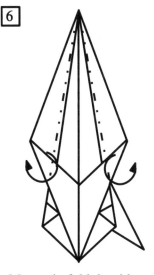

6

Mountain fold the sides into the model.

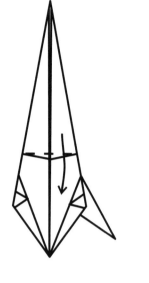

Valley fold the near flap down.

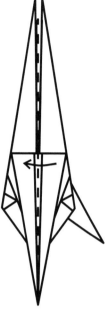

Valley fold the model in half.

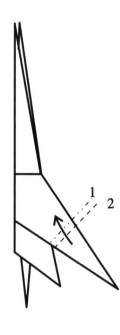

Form in order the
indicated reverse folds.

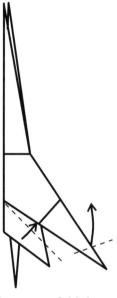

Outside reverse fold the nose up.
Outside reverse fold the mouth up.

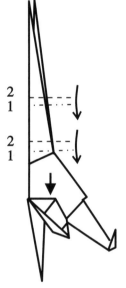

Form in order the indicated reverse folds.
Tuck the side of the jaw into the head.
Repeat behind.

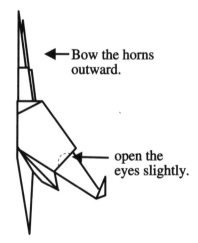

Bow the horns
outward.

open the
eyes slightly.

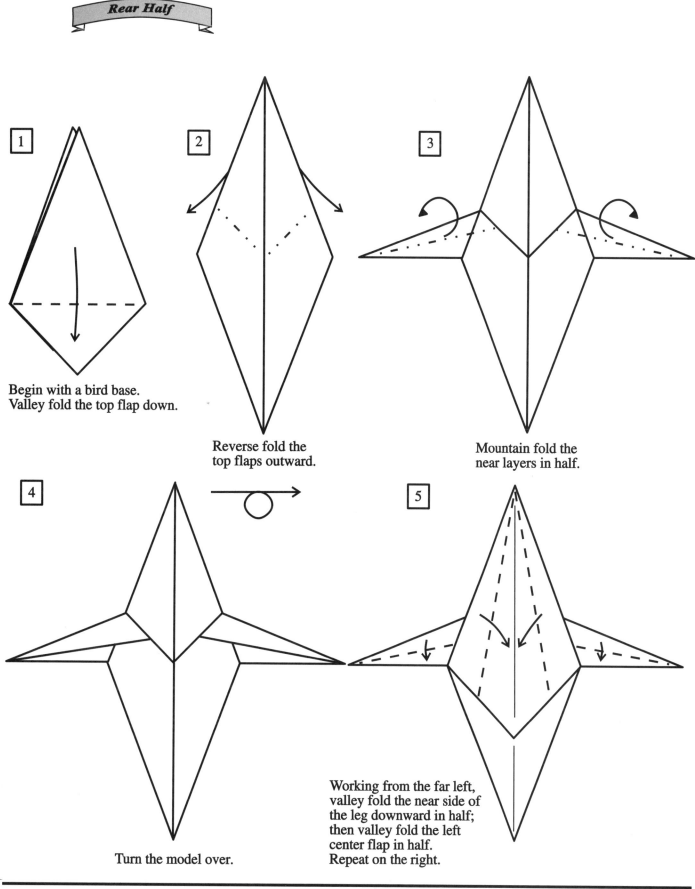

1

Begin with a bird base.
Valley fold the top flap down.

2

Reverse fold the
top flaps outward.

3

Mountain fold the
near layers in half.

4

Turn the model over.

5

Working from the far left,
valley fold the near side of
the leg downward in half;
then valley fold the left
center flap in half.
Repeat on the right.

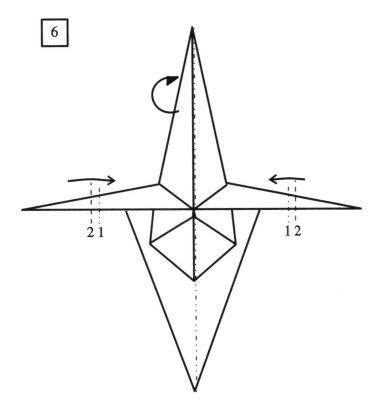

Form in order the indicated reverse folds.
Then mountain fold the model in half.

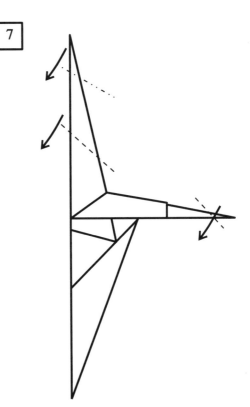

Outside reverse fold the large bend in the tail, then
inside reverse fold the tip of the tail as shown.
Outside reverse fold the tips of the side flaps to
form the feet.
Turn the model to the positon shown in step 8.

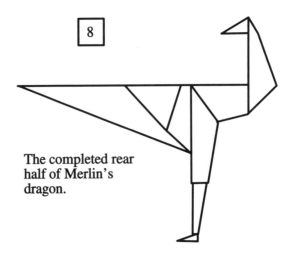

The completed rear
half of Merlin's
dragon.

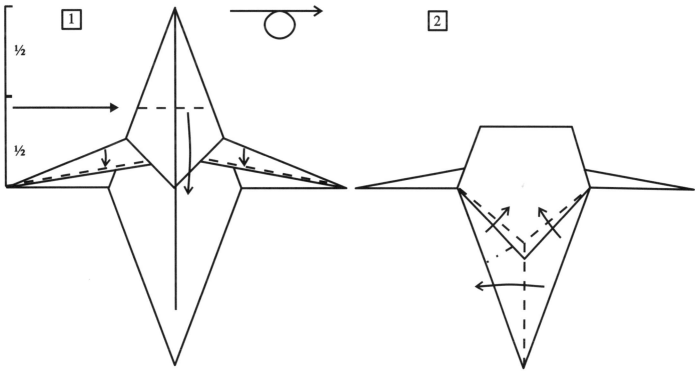

1

½

½

2

Begin with step 4 of the rear of the dragon.
Valley fold the top of the side flaps down inside the legs.
Valley fold more than half of the top flap down.
Turn the model over.

Fold the bottom flap into
a configuration of a rabbit-ear type.

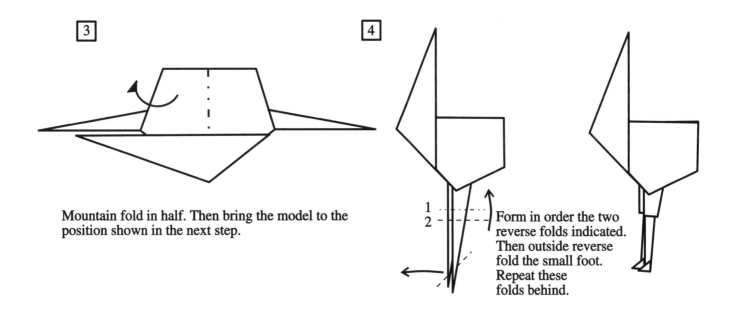

3

Mountain fold in half. Then bring the model to the
position shown in the next step.

4

1
2

Form in order the two
reverse folds indicated.
Then outside reverse
fold the small foot.
Repeat these
folds behind.

1

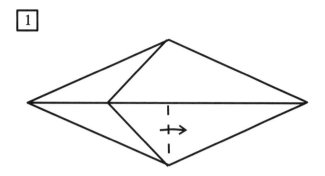

Begin with a fish base.
Valley fold the bottom flap
to the right as shown.

2

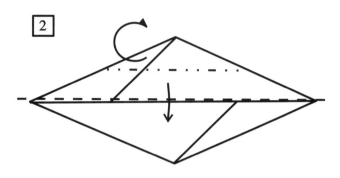

Mountain fold the top corner to the centerline in the back.
Then valley fold the base in half along the centerline.

3

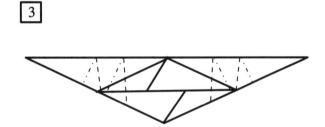

Crimp the wings as indicated.

4

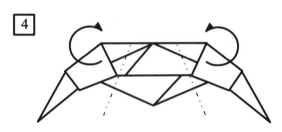

Mountain fold the wings.

5

Fold the model in half
and bring it to the position
shown in the next step.

6

The completed dragon's wings.

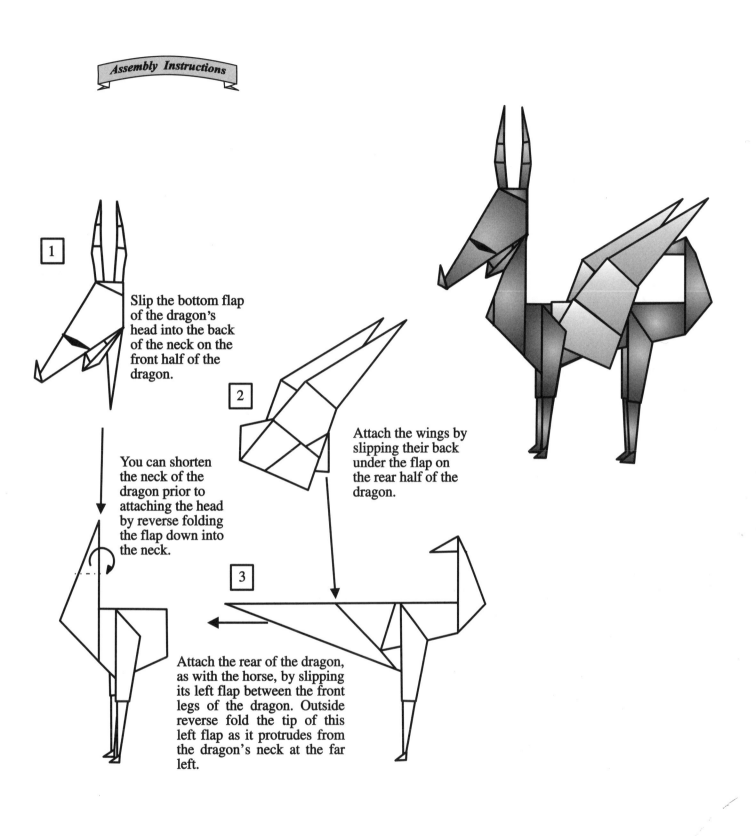

1

Slip the bottom flap of the dragon's head into the back of the neck on the front half of the dragon.

You can shorten the neck of the dragon prior to attaching the head by reverse folding the flap down into the neck.

2

Attach the wings by slipping their back under the flap on the rear half of the dragon.

3

Attach the rear of the dragon, as with the horse, by slipping its left flap between the front legs of the dragon. Outside reverse fold the tip of this left flap as it protrudes from the dragon's neck at the far left.

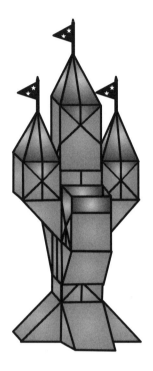 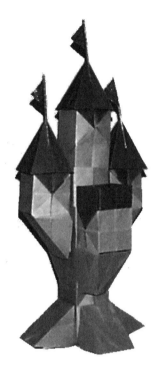

Merlin's tower is composed of 26 units assembled in much the same way as the fairy tale castle. All of the units except the support blocks and the connectors have already been used in the fairy tale castle. These basic models are simply joined in new ways to create Merlin's tower.

The tower is built on a single half building block steadied by four support blocks. This base assembly supports the complex tower structure.

The main tower is constructed of a base assembly, a lower tower assembly, and an upper tower assembly. These three assemblies hold side towers that are similar to the turrets of the fairy tale castle but much larger.

There are four side towers on the main tower assembly. One of these side towers has a tower top that can be used to hold Merlin as he looks out over his domain. Each of the other three side towers has a roof identical to the roof used on the fairy tale castle.

The following units are needed to assemble the base of Merlin's tower:
   4 support blocks
   2 half building blocks

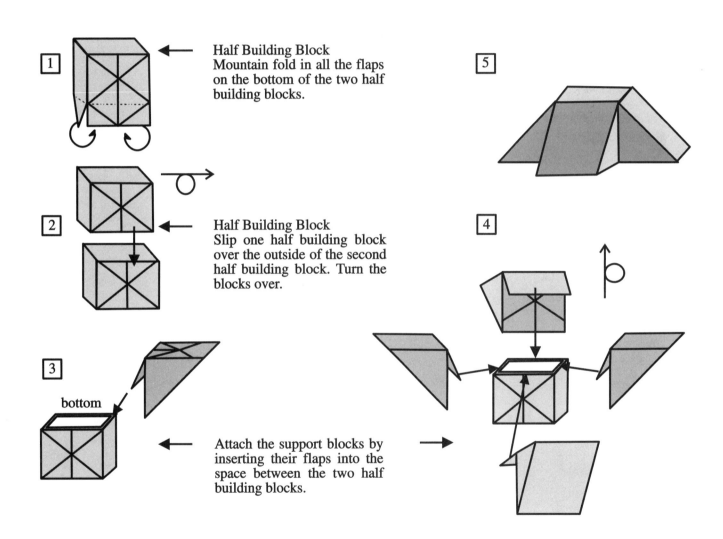

1

Half Building Block
Mountain fold in all the flaps on the bottom of the two half building blocks.

2

Half Building Block
Slip one half building block over the outside of the second half building block. Turn the blocks over.

3

bottom

Attach the support blocks by inserting their flaps into the space between the two half building blocks.

4

5

Lower Side Tower Assembly

The following units are needed to assemble the lower side tower supports:
  1 building block
  2 support blocks
  1 connector

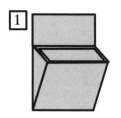 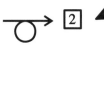 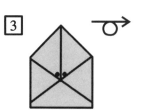 

1 Begin with a support block. Turn the model over.

2 Squash fold the top flaps down. Watch the black dots.

3 The unit now should have one pointed flap on top and two pointed flaps below.

4 The support block ready for assembly. Repeat steps 1–4 with the second support block.

5 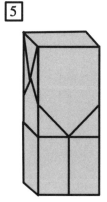 Slip a complete building block into a connector. Turn the assembly so that the building block has a flap pointing down as shown.

6 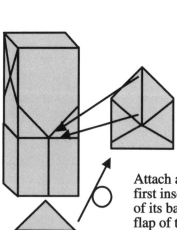 Attach a support block by first inserting the top point of its back flap under the flap of the building block. Next insert the two pointed flaps on the bottom of the support block into the connector. Repeat this procedure on the reverse side of the assembly.

7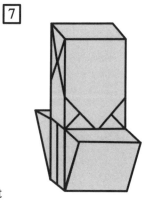

Lower Tower Assembly

The following units are needed to assemble the lower part of the tower:
- 1 connector
- 1 lower side tower assembly
- 1 half building block
- 1 tower base assembly

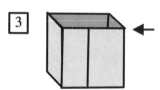

3

Connector
Slip the connector over the outside of the building block on the lower side tower assembly.

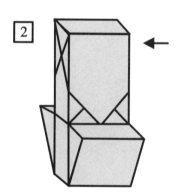

2

Lower Side Tower Assembly
Attach this assembly by slipping its connector over the outside of the half building block on the tower base assembly.

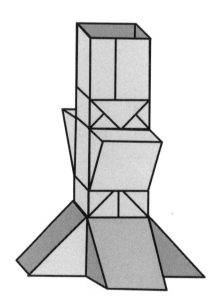

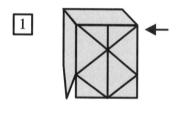

1

Half Building Block
Slip the flaps of the half building block over the half building block holding the support blocks on the base of the tower.

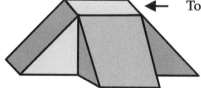

Tower Base Assembly

Upper Tower Assembly

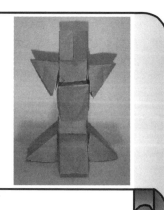

The following units are needed to assemble the upper tower:
  1 lower tower assembly
  2 support blocks

1

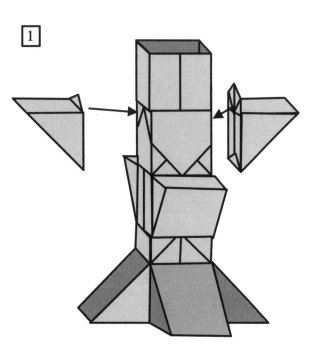

Attach the support blocks, in the same way as the lower tower assembly, by slipping the top flap under the connector. The two bottom flaps of the support blocks slip under the flap of the building block.

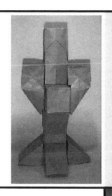

The following units are needed to assemble the upper side towers:
- 4 half building blocks
- 1 building block
- 1 upper tower assembly

1

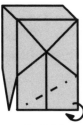

Mountain fold the side flap on a half building block up inside the model. Repeat behind, on the opposite diagonal.

2

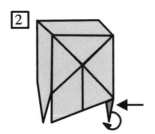

Mountain fold the pointed flap of the half building block up into the model as shown.

3

The completed half building block ready for assembly.

4

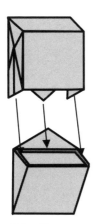

Insert the flaps on a half building block into the pockets formed in the support block.
Repeat steps 1–4 on the remaining half building blocks.
Don't forget the support block on the back of the tower.

5

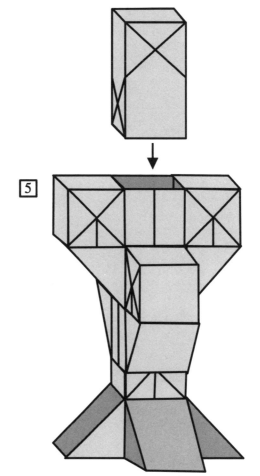

Insert the building block into the connector on the upper tower assembly.

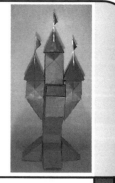

The following units are needed to assemble the finished tower:
4 roofs
1 tower top
1 upper side tower assembly

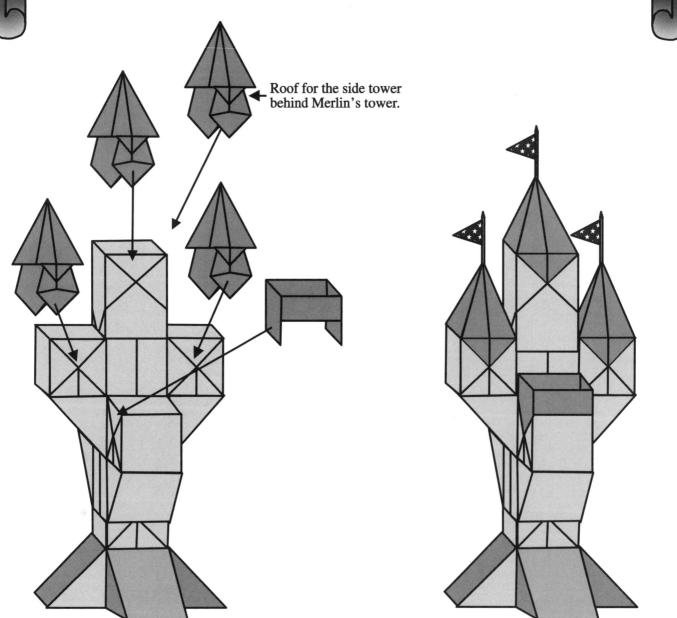

Roof for the side tower
behind Merlin's tower.

The drawings above show how to complete Merlin's tower. The drawing on the left, an exploded view of the tower, shows how to insert the lower flaps of the roof models into the half building blocks on the side towers. The roofs attach to the half building blocks in the same way as in the fairy tale castle. Don't forget the roof for the side tower in the rear of the tower. The lower flaps of the tower top insert into one of the half building blocks on a side tower. You can add flags and banners to finish Merlin's tower.

The Realm of Camelot

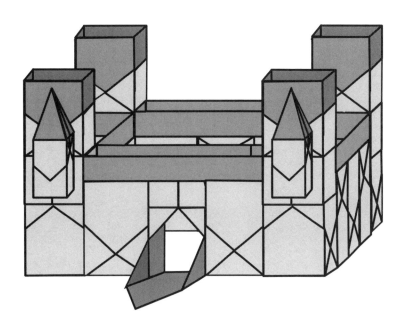

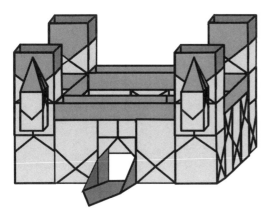

Camelot is composed of 58 units assembled in much the same way as the fairy tale castle. All of these units except the ramparts have already been used in the fairy tale castle and Merlin's tower; they are simply joined in new ways to create Camelot.

The construction uses four towers, which are like those of the fairy tale castle but extend higher and are topped with a small rampart, the tower top. You will find that the towers look better if you use a darker or brighter colored paper for the tower tops.

The back and side walls of Camelot are simply three complete building blocks fastened together by their pointed flaps. The front wall of the castle is different only in that an arched block forms a gatehouse between two of the building blocks. Make sure to carefully line up the pointed flaps exactly as they appear in the instructions, so that the units will fasten to each other properly. Unlike the fairy tale castle, these walls are not capped by tower tops; they are instead completed with long ramparts.

The ramparts used in the construction of Camelot are simple open-ended boxes folded together to make an adjustable box. You can lengthen or shorten these boxes to fit over any number of building blocks. Camelot uses only three building blocks for each wall, so the ramparts are rather short and hold the castle together fairly tightly. If you are careful, you can pick up the castle and move it from one location to another.

The drawbridge on the castle is the same as the one on the fairy tale castle; it can be folded up or down as you wish.

Tower Assembly

The following units are needed to assemble the tower:
    1 tower top
    1 half building block.
    1 connector
    1 building block.

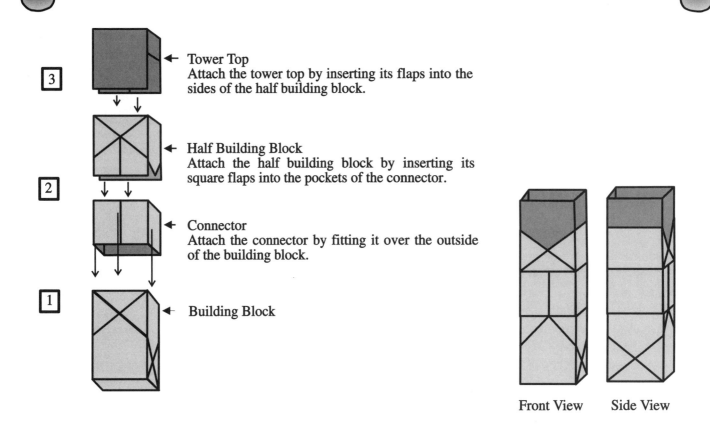

3 → Tower Top
Attach the tower top by inserting its flaps into the sides of the half building block.

2 → Half Building Block
Attach the half building block by inserting its square flaps into the pockets of the connector.

→ Connector
Attach the connector by fitting it over the outside of the building block.

1 → Building Block

Front View   Side View

The drawings above show an exploded view of the castle tower and two views of the completed tower. I have chosen to give you two views so you can see the location of the pointed flaps on the building blocks that are used to connect the parts of the castle. It is very important that you assemble the tower exactly as it appears in the drawings. In step 1, you slip the connector over the complete building block. The connector must be aligned with the folded side flaps facing you. You can see these flaps on the front view of the tower. In step 2, when you have the connector over the building block, insert all four flaps of a half building block into the pockets of the connector. In step 3, slip the flaps of the tower top into the side pockets of the half building block.

You will need to construct a total of 4 towers to complete Camelot.

Front Wall Assembly

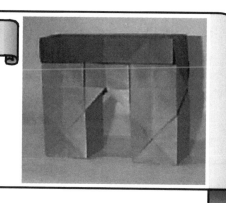

The following units are needed to assemble the front wall of Camelot:
- 2 complete building blocks
- 1 arched block
- 1 rampart

1

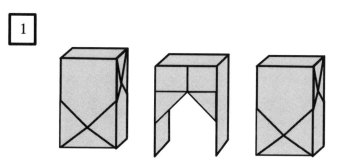

The front wall of Camelot ready for assembly.

2

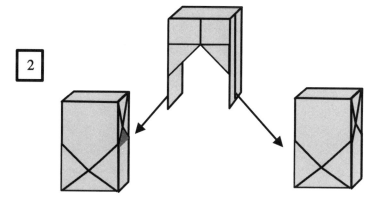

Insert the side flaps on the arched block into the pointed flaps on the building blocks.

3

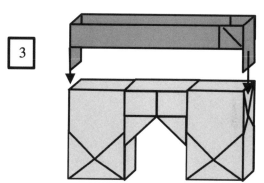

Insert the end flaps of the rampart into the sides of the outer building blocks.

4

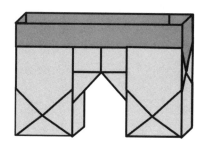

The front wall of Camelot assembled.

Arrange the models as shown in step 1, which is the view you would see if you were looking from the front of the castle. In step 2, you can see how to insert the side flaps of the arched block into the pointed flaps on the sides of the building blocks. The flaps have been shaded in the drawing to help locate them. Push the flaps of the arched block all the way down into the building blocks so that the top of the arched block is even with the top of the building blocks. Step 3 shows how to attach the rampart by inserting its end flaps into the sides of the outer building blocks.

The following units are needed to assemble the back wall of Camelot:
3 building blocks
1 rampart

1

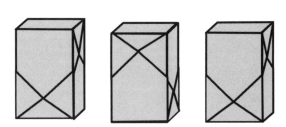

The back wall of Camelot ready for assembly.

2

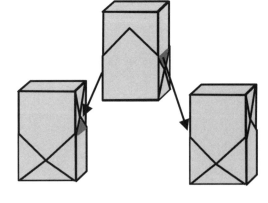

Insert the pointed flaps on the inner building block into the pointed flaps of the outer building blocks.

3

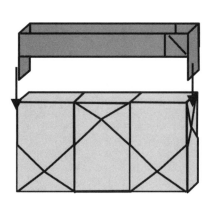

Insert the flaps on the end of the rampart into the sides of the outer blocks.

4

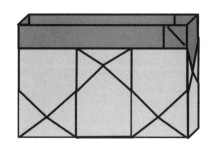

The back wall of Camelot assembled.

The following units are needed to assemble the sides of Camelot:
   3 complete building blocks

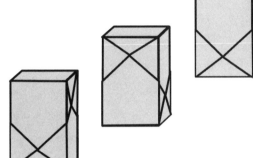

The side walls of Camelot ready for assembly.

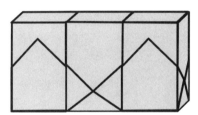

Side View

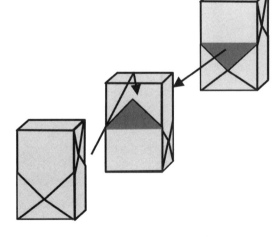

Insert the pointed flaps of the outer building blocks
into the side flaps of the center building block.

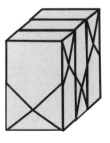

Front View

The following units are needed to assemble the back of Camelot:
  1 back wall assembly
  2 tower assemblies

1

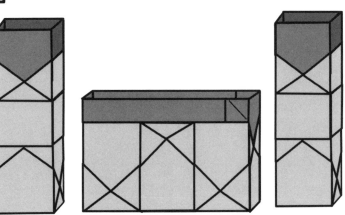

The back of the castle ready for assembly.

2

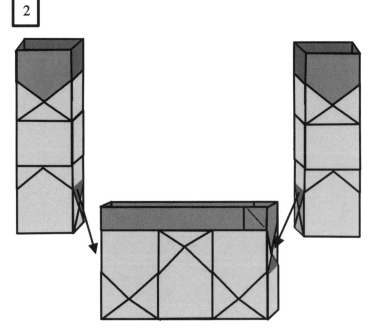

Insert the pointed flaps on the outer towers
into the pointed flaps of the building blocks.

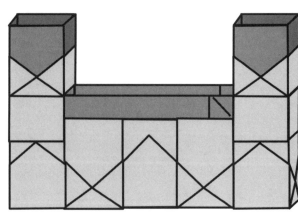

The back of the castle assembled.

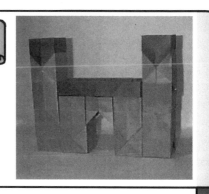

The following units are needed to assemble the front of Camelot:
  1 front wall assembly
  2 tower assemblies

1

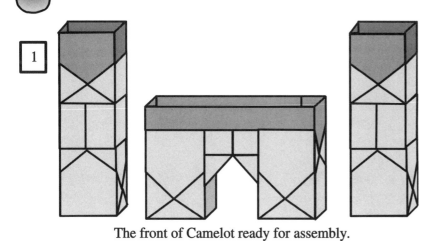

The front of Camelot ready for assembly.

2

3

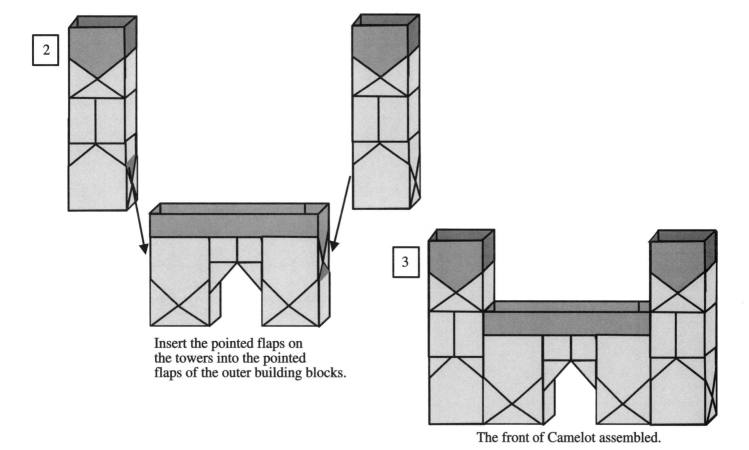

Insert the pointed flaps on
the towers into the pointed
flaps of the outer building blocks.

The front of Camelot assembled.

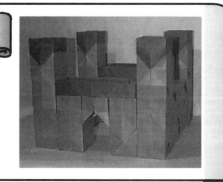

The following units are needed to complete the assembly of Camelot:
  1 front assembly
  1 back assembly
  2 side wall assemblies

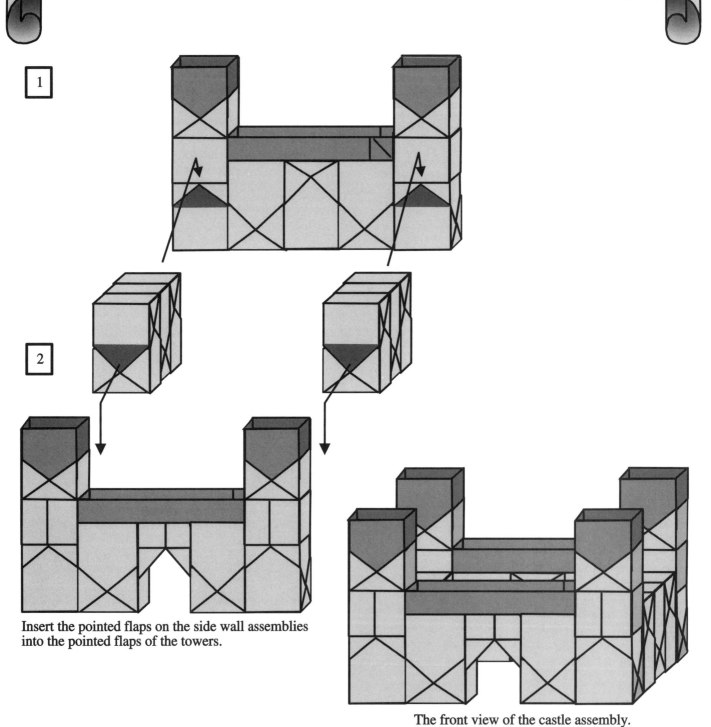

Insert the pointed flaps on the side wall assemblies into the pointed flaps of the towers.

The front view of the castle assembly.

Camelot Assembly

The following units are needed to complete the assembly of Camelot:
- 1 castle assembly
- 2 ramparts

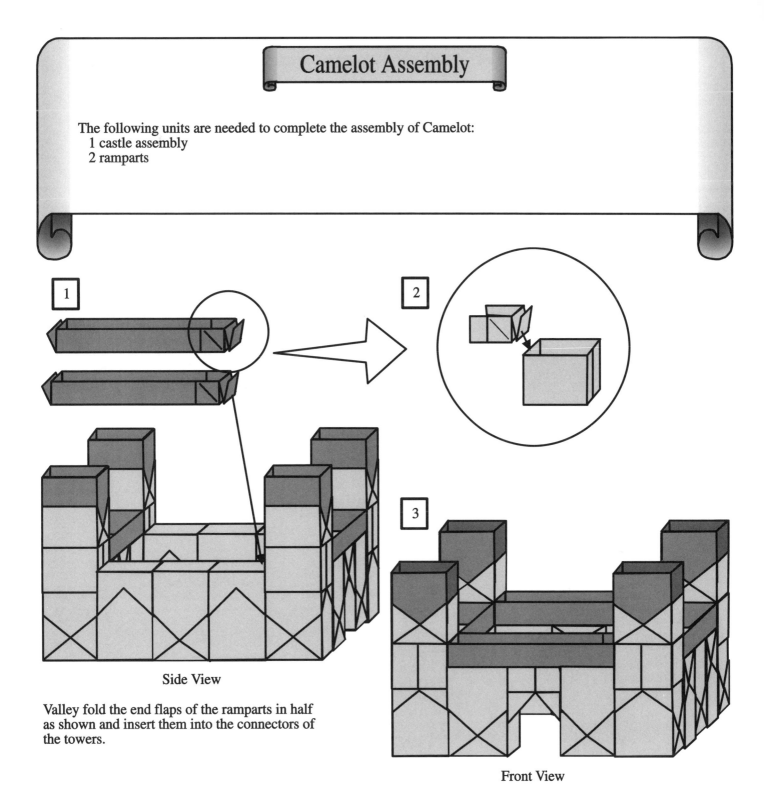

1

2

3

Side View

Front View

Valley fold the end flaps of the ramparts in half as shown and insert them into the connectors of the towers.

Turn the castle assembly so that the side is facing you as in step 1. Carefully insert the end flaps of a rampart into the pockets of the tower connectors. This can be accomplished more easily if the side flaps on the ramparts are valley folded in half. Gently coax the flaps into the connectors until the rampart sits on top of the side walls. Step 2 shows how to insert the shortened flap into the side of the connector. This drawing has been simplified to show only the rampart flap and the connector. Step 3 shows how the Camelot assembly looks from the front.

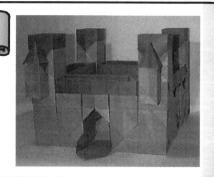

The following units are needed for final assembly of Camelot:
   1 Camelot assembly
   1 drawbridge
   2 castle turrets found in the fairy tale castle

1

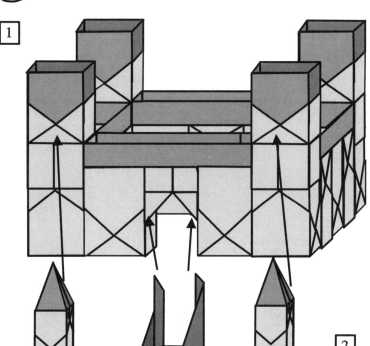

Insert the drawbridge into the arched block on the front of Camelot. Attach the turrets to the front towers of Camelot.

2

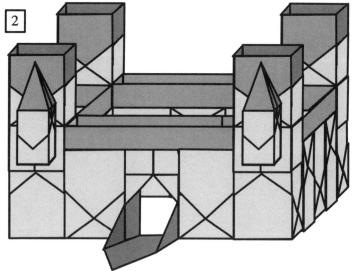

Align Camelot so that the front of the model faces you. Step 1 shows how to insert the drawbridge into the arched block on the front of Camelot. This is the same assembly as the fairy tale castle. Hang the two turrets from the connectors on the front towers by the pointed flaps on the back of each turret. Step 2 shows Camelot with all the units in place. You may want to add a total of eight turrets to Camelot to make it look more like the fairy tale castle.

King Arthur Pendragon

Fold King Arthur Pendragon by making a knight from two 4″ square sheets of the laminated paper described below, a knight's sword from a 2″ square sheet of paper, and Merlin's cloak from a 4″ sheet of paper. You will also need a 4″ x ½″ rectangular sheet of paper for King Arthur's staff and four 1½″ square sheets of paper for the staff's dragon head, King Arthur's crown, Excalibur, and Excalibur's scabbard. Try using silver foil paper for the swords, gold foil paper for the crown, and brightly colored paper for the cloak.

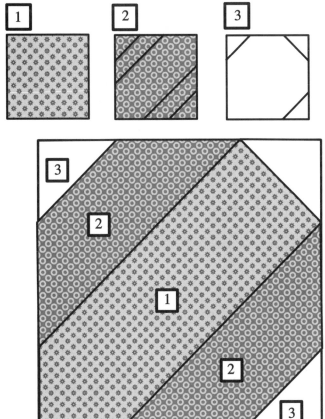

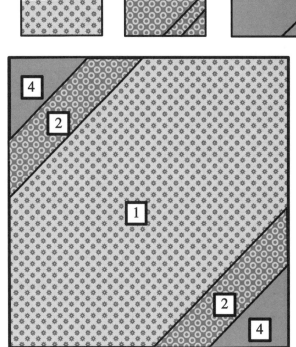

Top half of the model

Bottom half of the model

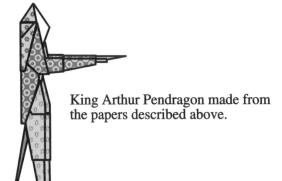

King Arthur Pendragon made from the papers described above.

The drawings above show how to laminate paper for King Arthur. The different papers have been cut and glued to a primary sheet of paper. Paper 1 is the primary sheet of paper. Paper 2 is a second sheet of paper cut and glued to the primary sheet of paper. Papers 3 and 4 are flesh-colored paper and paper of black or brown for King Arthur's boots.

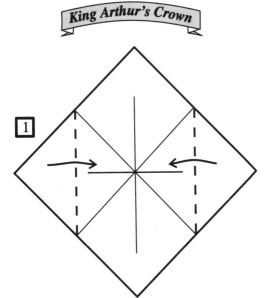

1 Begin with an unfolded waterbomb base. Valley fold opposite corners to the center.

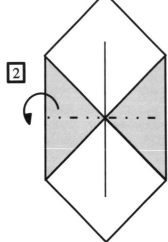

2 Mountain fold the paper in half.

3 Reverse fold the opposite corners in to the centerline.

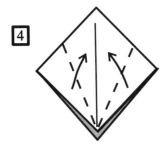

4 Valley fold the corners to the centerline. Repeat behind.

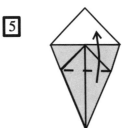

5 Valley fold the top flap up. Do **not** repeat behind.

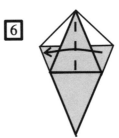

6 Valley fold the near flap in half along the centerline.

7 Mountain fold the far flap in half back.

8 Open up the model and bend the outside flaps down slightly.

9 The completed crown.

1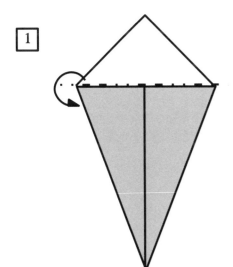

Begin with a kite base.
Mountain fold the top back.

2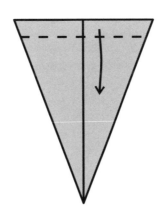

Valley fold the top of the
paper as shown.

3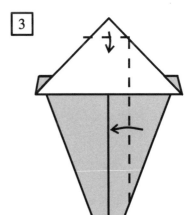

Valley fold the tip of the paper.
Valley fold the right side of the
paper across the centerline.

4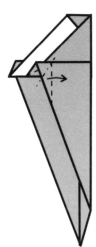

Pull the edge to the right
and squash the corner into
the small collar shown in
step 5.

5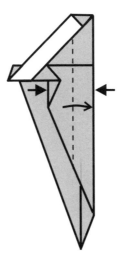

Valley fold the top layer of paper
so that the left edge is even with
the right edge.
The edges are indicated by the
large pointed arrows.

6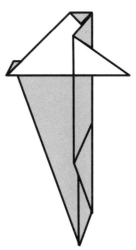

The model should look
like this.

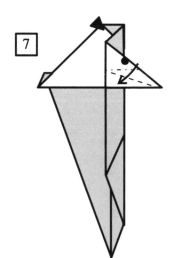

7

Pull the raw edge downward,
bisecting the right corner, and
squash the upper corner into
the collar shown in step 8. Watch
the black dot.

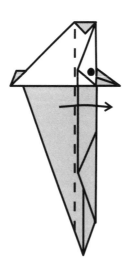

8

Valley fold the left
half of the paper
across the centerline.

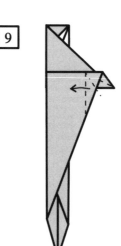

9

Repeat step 4 by
pulling the edge to
the left and squashing
the corner.

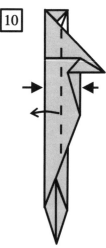

10

Repeat step 5 by
valley folding the
paper back.

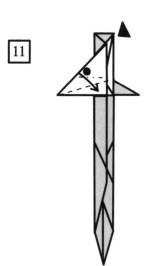

11

Repeat step 7 by pulling the raw
edge downward to bisect the left
corner; squash the upper corner into
the collar shown in step 12. Watch
the black dot.

12

The sword should
look like this.
Turn the model over.

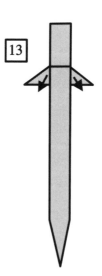

13

Pull out the small
flaps just under the
top layers of paper.
Wrap these flaps around
the front of the sword.

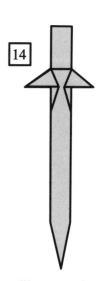

14

Excalibur completed.

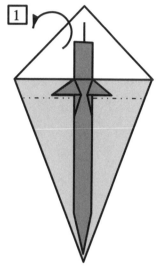

1 Begin with a kite base. Place the model of Excalibur on the centerline of the paper. Mountain fold the kite base just below the hilt of Excalibur. Unfold the paper and remove the model of Excalibur.

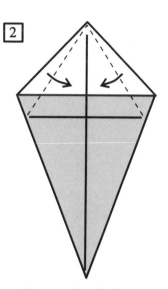

2 Form valley folds that run from the tip of the kite to the ends of the crease made in step 1.

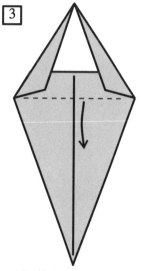

3 Pull down and flatten the two small internal flaps.

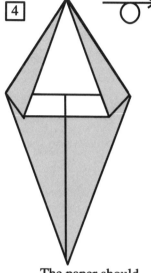

4 The paper should look like this. Turn the model over.

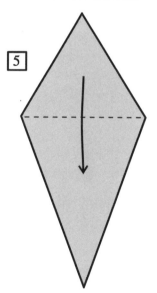

5 Valley fold the top downward.

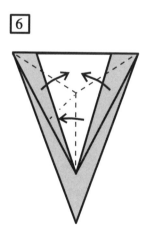

6 Form a rabbit ear.

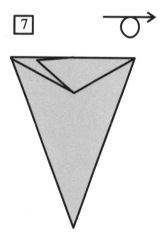

7 Turn the model over.

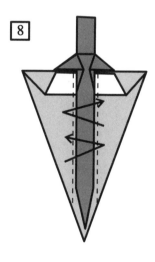

8 Place Excalibur on the paper and valley fold the sides of the paper over the blade. Unfold. Leave extra room on both sides.

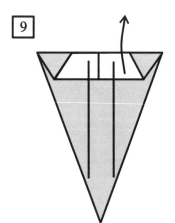

9

Remove the model
of Excalibur.
Fold the right flap
upward.

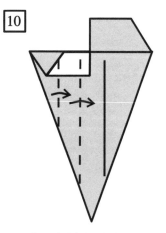

10

Valley fold the left corner
to the crease line made in
step 8.
Then valley fold on the
crease line made in step 8.

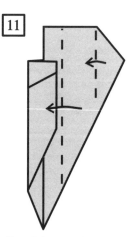

11

Valley fold the right corner
to the crease line made in
step 8.
Then valley fold on the
crease line made in step 8.

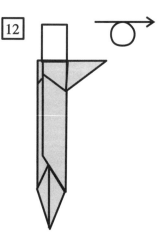

12

Turn the scabbard over.

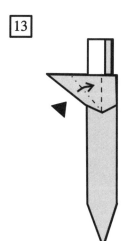

13

Lift the sharp flap and
squash fold it upward.

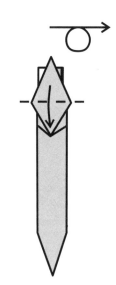

14

Valley fold the top flap
down.
Turn the model over.

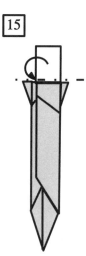

15

Mountain fold the top flap
down into the central tube, just
in front of the rabbit ear fold.
Do not fold it into the rabbit
ear.

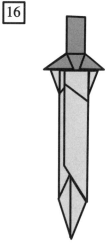

16

Excalibur should
slip easily into the
scabbard.

1 Roll up the paper about halfway on a toothpick.

2 Slide the toothpick out of the paper.

3 Continue to roll the paper until it is very tight.

4 The completed shaft for King Arthur's staff.

5

6

Fold the small dragon-head.
Unroll the staff far enough to insert the flap on the head of the dragon. Roll up the staff with the dragon's head at the end. Fold the hand of a king's attendant or King Arthur to hold the staff. Insert the staff into the hand.

1

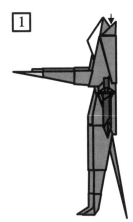

You can attach Excalibur by inserting the flap on the back of the scabbard into the pocket on the side of King Arthur. You will need to keep the extra knight's sword in order for the model to stand up by itself. There is a small flap behind the king's head; reverse fold it straight down to the right.

2

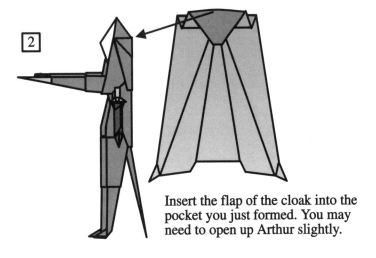

Insert the flap of the cloak into the pocket you just formed. You may need to open up Arthur slightly.

3

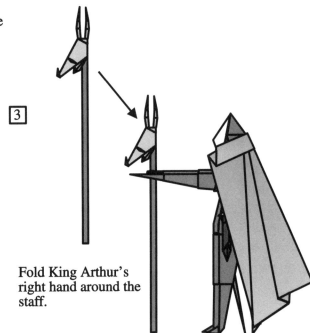

Fold King Arthur's right hand around the staff.

4

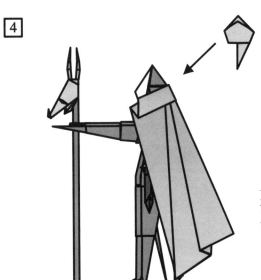

Insert the flap on the bottom of the crown into the side of the same pocket.

5

Fold Queen Guinevere by making a knight base from a 4″ square sheet of paper, an eight-sided cone from a 4″ square sheet of the laminated paper described below, and Merlin's cloak from a 3″ square sheet of paper. Guinevere's hat is made from two more sheets of paper: a 1½″ square and a ½″ square.

Lower Half

The lower half of Queen Guinevere is made from an eight-sided cone. Follow the directions for the eight-sided cone. If you have used a foil-backed doily, you can mold the cone into a round shape.

The drawings above show how to laminate Queen Guinevere's dress with a doily. Be sure to use a paper that is fairly thin for the laminate. If you use a round paper, try to center it as much as possible. There are many different types of paper doily to choose from. Some are beautiful foil papers that make the dress look fantastic.

1

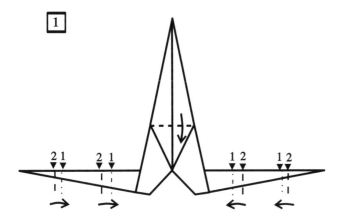

Begin with a knight base. Valley fold the top flap down. Form the elbows and wrists by making in order the pairs of reverse folds indicated.

2

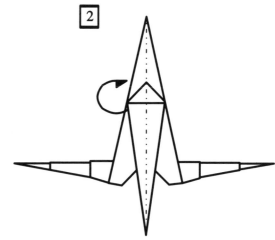

Mountain fold the paper in half.

3

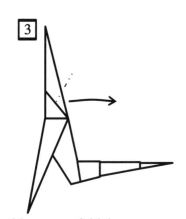

Inside reverse fold the top point.

4

Outside reverse fold the end of the flap. Outside reverse fold again to form the head and face. Then reverse fold straight down to the left the small flap to the left of the head.

5

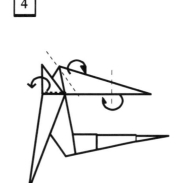

The upper half of Queen Guinevere.

1

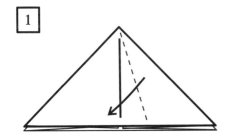

Begin with a waterbomb base.
Valley fold the top right flap diagonally
about one third the length of the
bottom edge of the paper.

2

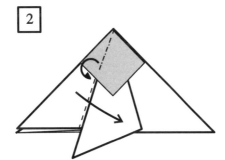

Place the small square of paper
on the waterbomb base as shown.
Mountain fold the edge of the
small paper under the top flap of
the base. Valley fold the opposite
flap of the waterbomb base over
both the flap and the small sheet
of paper.

3

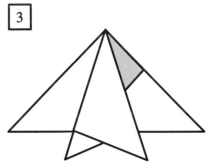

Repeat the diagonal
folds in steps 1–2 behind.

4

Mountain fold and unfold the near
top layer.
Valley fold the bottom flaps up
to the crease line.
Repeat behind.

5

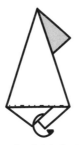

Mountain fold the bottom flaps
up into the pocket behind them.
Be careful to get both flaps
between the layers.
Repeat behind.

6

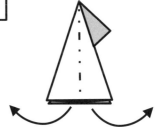

Open out the hat from
beneath and flatten it.

7

When the model is opened, it
will form a hat with a small
flap at the top.

Queen Guinevere's Hat
Attach the hat by placing it over Queen Guinevere's head. Or you may wish to use a crown like that of King Arthur.

Upper Half of Queen Guinevere
Attach the upper half of the queen by inserting its vertical flap into one of the pockets in the eight-sided cone. This flap must go behind both layers of paper. The pocket of the cone will open up as you slide the flap into it.

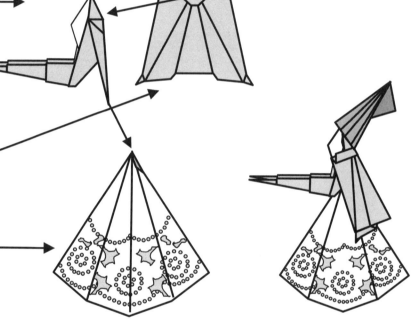

Queen Guinevere's Cape (Merlin's Cloak)
Attach the small cape worn by Queen Guinevere in the same way as you attached the cloak to Merlin.

Queen Guinevere's Skirt
The queen's skirt has two pockets formed by the folds in the model. These pockets provide spaces to attach the upper half of Queen Guinevere, but you will need only one of them.

The above drawings show an exploded view of Queen Guinevere and a completed model. Use a toothpick to open up one of the pockets in Guinevere's skirt. This will allow you to insert the flap of the upper half of Queen Guinevere. Open the cone enough to insert the flap under both folds in the **back** of the eight-sided cone; the cone will open slightly as you insert the flap. Slide the upper half of Queen Guinevere down into the eight-sided cone. After you are satisfied with this portion of the assembly, crease the upper half of the queen along the centerline. This will help hold it in place and improve the appearance of the model.

Court Jester

Fold the court jester by making a knight from two 4″ square sheets of the laminated paper described below, a knight's sword from a 2″ square sheet of paper, and a knight's upper half from a 1½″ square sheet of paper (the puppet). You will need another 1½″ square sheet for the jester's hat.

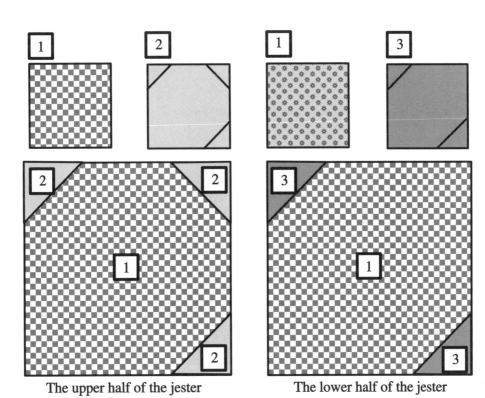

The upper half of the jester

The lower half of the jester

The court jester should be folded from a paper with a small square pattern or from a paper with a small bright pattern. Reverse fold the small flap in back of the head down in the same way as you did in the folding of Queen Guinevere. This will allow the jester to wear a jester's hat.

The drawings above show a laminant with a very small square pattern. Tissue paper can be used to laminate an origami paper or a paper with foil on one side. Foil-backed papers tend to keep their shape longer than other papers. Tissue paper is very thin and does not interfere with folding. The small triangles on the corners of the above sheets are flesh-colored paper on the upper half of the court jester and black or brown paper on the lower half of the court jester.

 1

Begin with a preliminary fold.
Valley fold the near flap up and
bring it back down.

 2

Form the near flap into
a rabbit ear.

3

Valley fold the near flap up.

4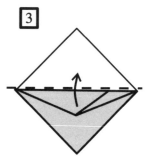

Repeat steps 1–3 on both the
right and left inside flaps.
Turn the model over.

5

Valley fold the sides to
the centerline.

6

Swing the near right
flap to the left.

7

Valley fold the edge of the
right flap down to the centerline.

8

Swing two left flaps
to the right.

9

Valley fold the edge of the
left flap down to the centerline.

10

Insert a finger under the
inner flap and push it out.

11

The completed hat

Insert the long flap of the hat into the pocket on the side of the court jester's head. Open the hat enough to be placed over the head as you slide the flap down into the pocket. The two large flaps on the front of the hat should be opened out once the hat is in place.

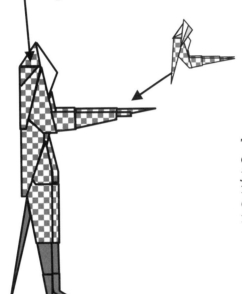

The jester's puppet is simply a small upper half of the jester himself. You may try to make a small jester's hat for the puppet, but you will have to fold it using a toothpick. Fold the hand of the court jester to hold the puppet. Insert the lower flap of the puppet into the hand of the court jester.

You may wish to bend up the toes of the court jester to resemble the soft felt shoes often worn by these court clowns.

The Sword in the Stone

Fold the stone from a 2″ square sheet of paper. The sword is Excalibur folded from a 1½″ square sheet.

 1

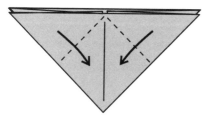

Begin with a waterbomb base. Valley fold the side flaps to the bottom. Repeat behind.

2

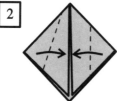

Valley fold the near layers to the centerline as shown. Repeat behind.

3

Fold the bottom right flap upward.

4

Tuck the bottom flaps up into the pockets in the folded sides and flatten. Repeat steps 2-4 behind.

5

Valley fold the bottom point up and back down.

6

Blow air into the top of the paper to inflate it.

7

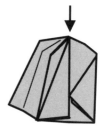

The completed stone. There is a small hole in the top of the model.

Assembly Instructions

Assemble the sword in the stone by inserting Excalibur into the hole in the top of the stone.

Fold the Round Table from an 8″ square sheet of paper. The table's base is an arched block folded from a 6″ square.

1

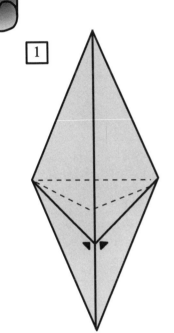

Fold a waterbomb base then unfold it.
Fold a fish base from the same
sheet of paper.
Squash fold the center flaps.

2

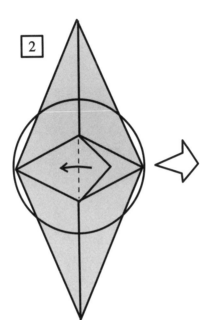

Valley fold the left near central
flap to the left along the centerline.
Repeat on the right center flap.
Steps 3–9 will show an
enlarged view of the center.

3

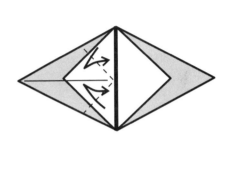

Valley fold the top and
bottom points to the
horizontal centerline.
Unfold these folds.

4

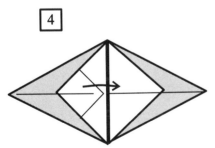

Swing the left near flap
to the right.

5

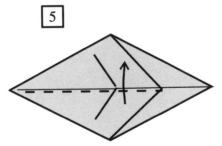

Valley fold the center flap
in half upward.

6

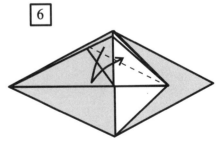

Valley fold the near top corner
of the center flap to the centerline
and unfold.

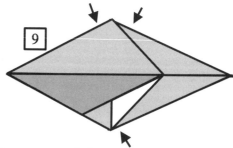

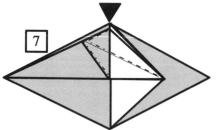

7 Inside reverse fold the near top corner downward.

8 Fold the top flap back down.

9 Repeat steps 5–8 on the uper half of the central flap. Then repeat steps 5–9 on the right central flap, so that the right matches the left.

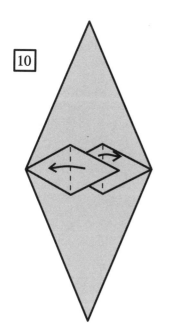

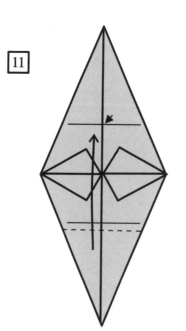

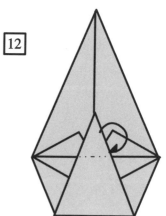

10 Valley fold the two center flaps in half as shown.

11 Valley fold the bottom point up to the crease left by the waterbomb folds.

12 Mountain fold the top of the flap along the horizontal centerline.

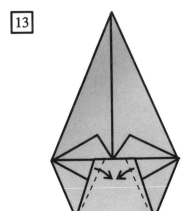

13

Valley fold the sides of the
near flap toward the centerline.

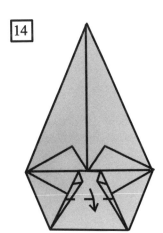

14

Valley fold the near flap
as shown, leaving it at right
angles to the rest of the table.
Repeat steps 12–14 on
the opposite flap.

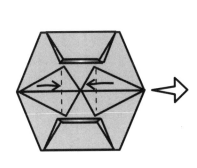

15

Valley fold the center flaps
up as shown, leaving them
at right angles to the table.

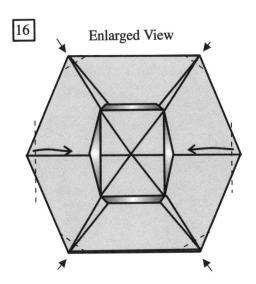

16   Enlarged View

Inside reverse fold the four corners on
the top and bottom of the table as shown.
Valley fold the left and right corners as shown.

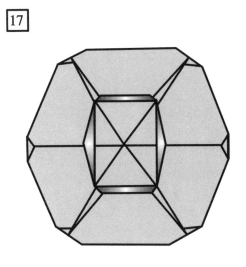

17

The four center flaps should all be pointing toward you

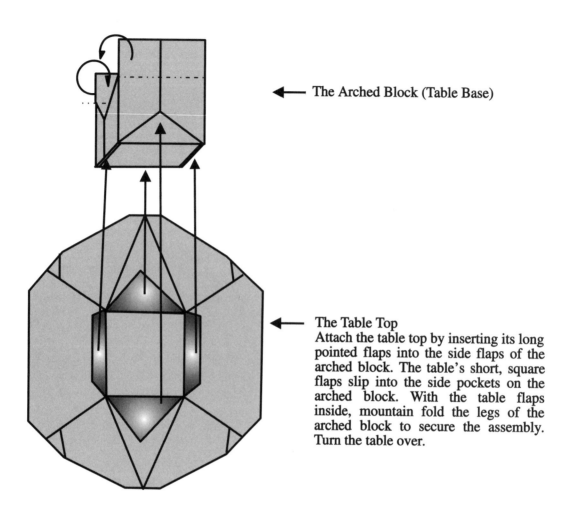

← The Arched Block (Table Base)

← The Table Top
Attach the table top by inserting its long pointed flaps into the side flaps of the arched block. The table's short, square flaps slip into the side pockets on the arched block. With the table flaps inside, mountain fold the legs of the arched block to secure the assembly. Turn the table over.

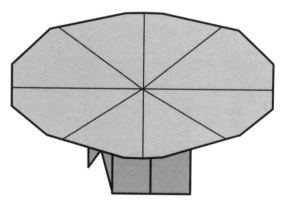

Chair

Fold the chair back from a 4″ square sheet of paper. The chair's base is an arched block also folded from a 4″ square.

1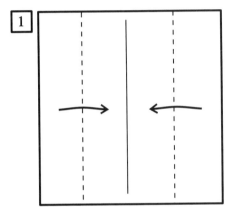

Valley fold the sides of the paper to the centerline.

2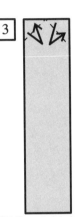

Valley fold the paper in half along the centerline.

3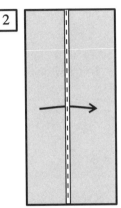

Valley fold the top corners at 45 degrees. Unfold the paper.

4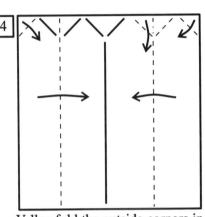

Valley fold the outside corners in along the crease line made in step 3.

Valley fold the right half of the paper in to the centerline as you pull down the small triangle made in step 3, forming a small reverse fold. Valley fold the left side to the centerline.

5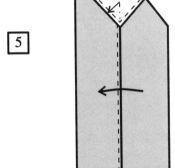

The paper should look like this. Valley fold the paper in half on the centerline. As you make this fold, pull down the small white triangle (forming a reverse fold) and tuck it behind the top layer of paper on the left. This will lock the chair back together in the next step.

6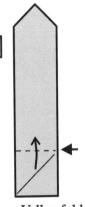

Tuck the top left flap down into the adjacent pocket. Valley fold the bottom corner along the diagonal and unfold.

7

Valley fold the bottom of the paper at the crease mark.

8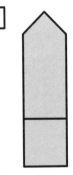

The finished chair back.

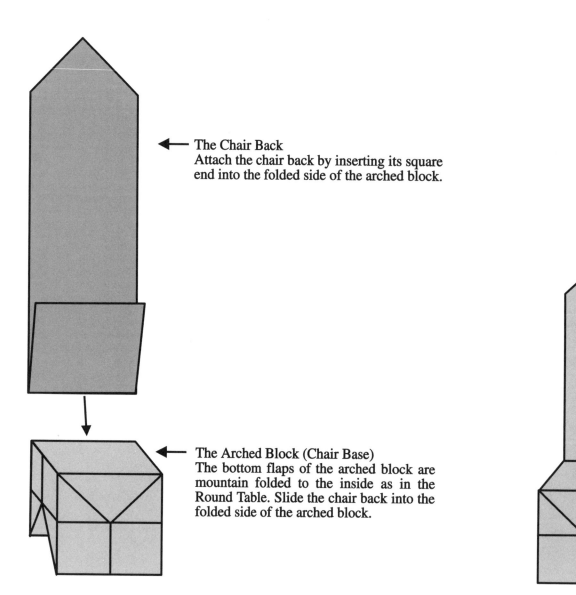

The Chair Back
Attach the chair back by inserting its square end into the folded side of the arched block.

The Arched Block (Chair Base)
The bottom flaps of the arched block are mountain folded to the inside as in the Round Table. Slide the chair back into the folded side of the arched block.

1

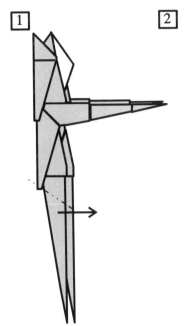

Unfold the knees and feet
of a knight.
Reverse fold the flap along the
diagonal as shown.

2

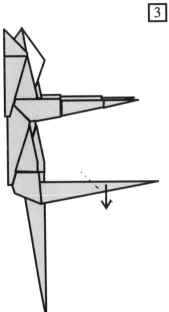

Reverse fold the flap
along the diagonal as
shown to form the knee.

3

Reverse fold the flap
to form the foot.
Repeat steps 1–3 on
the reverse side.

4

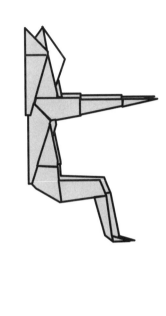

The completed folds.

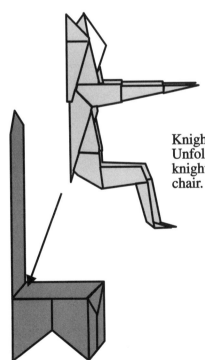

Knight of the Round Table
Unfold the flap on the lower half of the
knight and insert it into the back of a
chair.

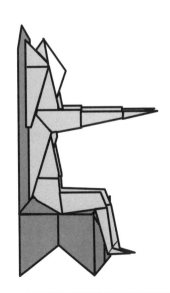

Throne

Fold the throne back from a 4″ x 6″ rectangular sheet of paper. The throne's base is an arched block folded from a 4″ square.

Throne Back

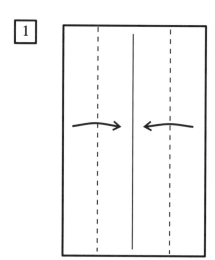

1. Valley fold the sides to the centerline.

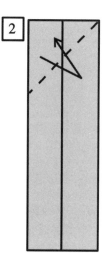

2. Valley fold the top right corner in half. Unfold.

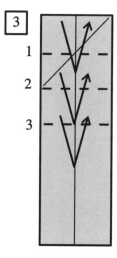

3. 1 Valley fold the top to the left tip of the crease made in step 2.
2 Valley fold along the crease made in step 2.
3 Valley fold once more, along the lower folded edge just formed. Unfold all three folds.

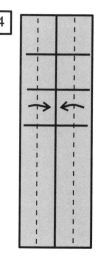

4. Valley fold the sides to the centerline.

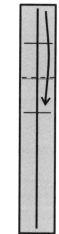

5. Valley fold the top down along the second crease line formed in step 3.

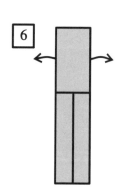

6. Pull outward the near inner edge, and flatten the model.

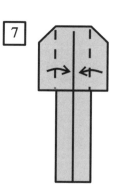

7. Valley fold the sides to the centerline.

8. Valley fold the near flap upward.

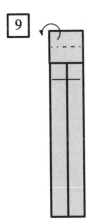

9

Mountain fold the top,
tucking it down into
the two triangular pockets
visible in the previous step.

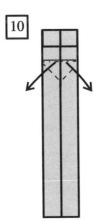

10

Pull outward the central edges at the
third crease line formed in step 3, and
pinch to set the canopy into its
horizontal position.

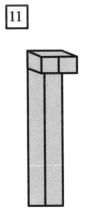

11

The throne back,
with a canopy.

Assembly Instructions

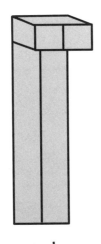

Throne Back
Attach the throne back by inserting
its square end into the folded side of
the arched block.

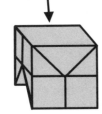

The Arched Block
The bottom flaps of the
arched block are mountain
folded into its inside.

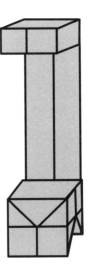

Throne 129

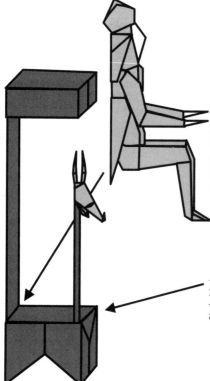

King Arthur and His Knights of the Round Table
Reverse fold the legs of King Arthur into
a sitting position. Unfold the flap on the lower
half of the king and insert it into the back of a
chair.

King Arthur's Staff
Insert the staff into the side of the
arched block.

The Royal Hunt

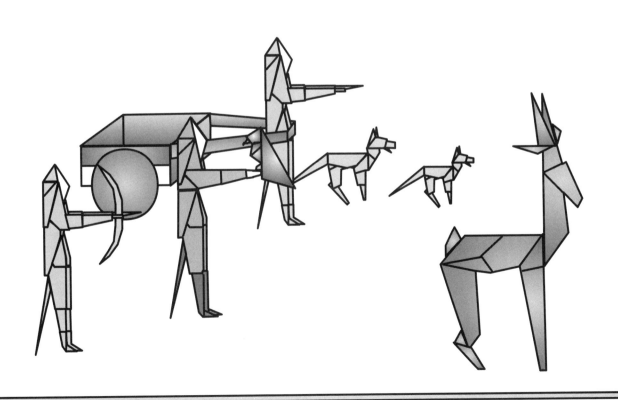

King's Falcon

Fold the falcon from a 2″ square sheet of paper.

1

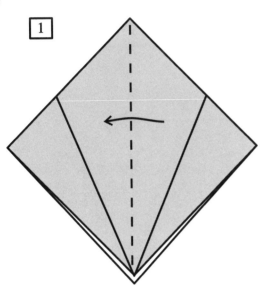

Begin with a bird base.
Unfold the back.
Valley fold the near flap
in half to the left.

2

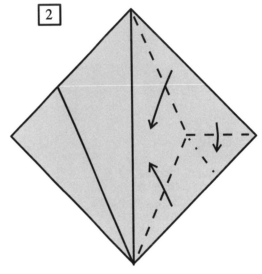

Form only the nearest single
layer into a rabbit ear.

3

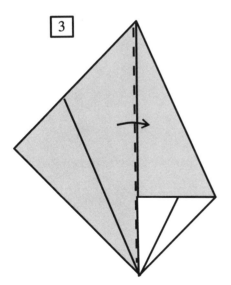

Swing to the right the two near left flaps.
Repeat step 2 on the opposite flap.

4

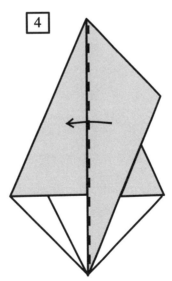

Swing the near flap
to the left.

5

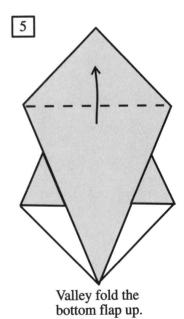

Valley fold the
bottom flap up.

King's Falcon 133

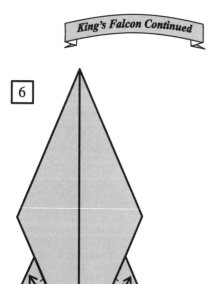

6

Fold exactly in half the near single layer of the small colored triangle at the left; run the crease upward as far as possible; repeat on the right.

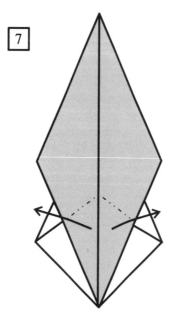

7

Reverse fold the colored flaps outward. The apex of these creases lies on the apex of the creases formed in step 6.

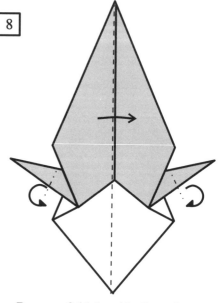

8

Reverse fold the side flaps down. Valley fold the paper in half along the centerline.

9

Crimp the top flap down over the outside as shown.

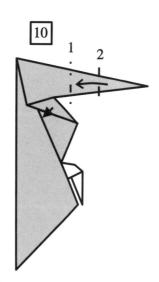

10

Form in order the two reverse folds indicated to make the head. Tuck the head under the wings on both front and back.

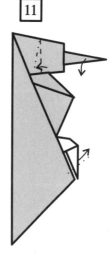

11

Crimp the head inward to form a hood. Bend the paper on the head to form the beak. Reverse fold the feet as shown. Repeat behind.

12

The completed king's falcon.

White Hart

Fold the white hart from two 4" square sheets of paper.

1

Begin with a bird base.
Valley fold the near flap up.
Repeat behind.

2

Valley fold the sides to the centerline.
Repeat behind.

3

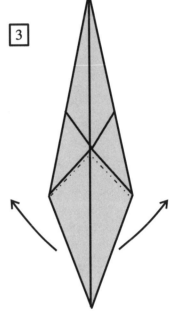

Reverse fold the bottom flaps outward.

4

Valley fold the near lower flaps upward.

5

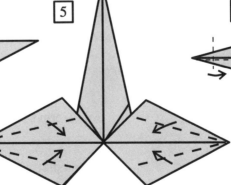

Valley fold the sides of the two flaps to the centerline.

6

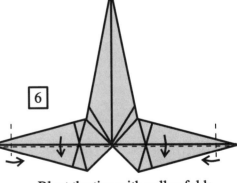

Blunt the tips with valley folds.
Valley fold both lower flaps downward in half.

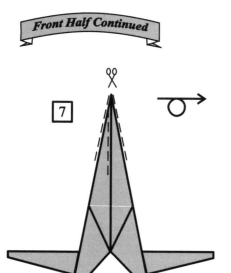

7

Slit the near flap along the
sides and centerline.
Turn the paper over.

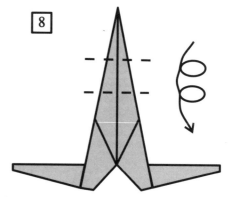

8

Valley fold the near flap
downward twice as shown.

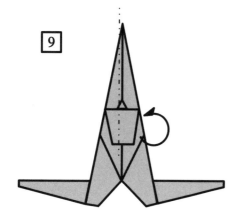

9

Mountain fold the paper in half.

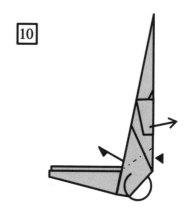

10

Mountain fold the near leg, twisting the chest
inward as the leg becomes vertical. Repeat behind
at the same time.
Pull out the head until the model looks like step 11.

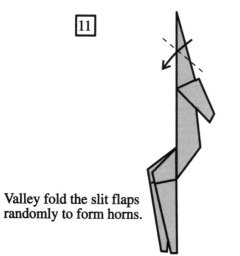

11

Valley fold the slit flaps
randomly to form horns.

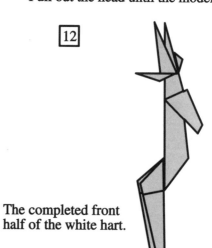

12

The completed front
half of the white hart.

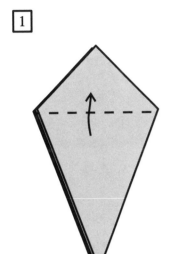

1

Begin with a bird base.
Valley fold the near flap up.
Do **not** repeat behind.

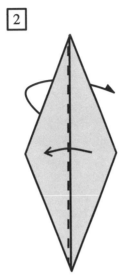

2

Fold the near flap in
half to the left.
Swivel the back flap
to the right.

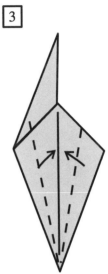

3

Valley fold the sides
to the centerline.
Repeat behind.

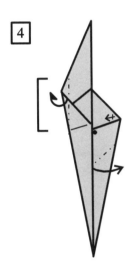

4

Mountain fold the left corner
inward: this mountain fold is
vertical, and its lower end touches
the left end of an existing crease.
Working from the bottom, swing the
right inner edge to the right,
swivelling its upper part into the
position shown in step 5; watch the
black dot. (The bracketed distance in
step 5 is the same as the bracketed
distance in step 4.) Flatten the
model, and repeat behind.

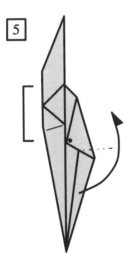

5

Reverse fold the right flap
upward as far as possible; treat
the small triangular area just
below the mountain fold line as
part of the flap, as if the flap
were a single thickness.
Swivel the lower part of the flap
with mountain folds as you do
the reverse fold.

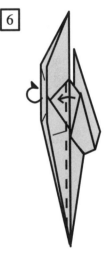

6

Swing the far left flap to
the right. Then swing the
near right flap to the left.

7

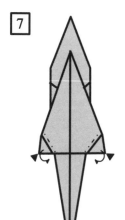

Reverse fold the
lower corners.

8

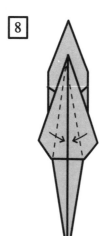

Valley fold the sides
of the near flap to
the centerline.

9

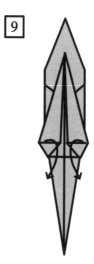

Swivel the two
small collars into
the positon shown
in step 10.

10

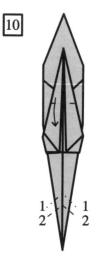

Valley fold the near flap down
to begin formation of the tail.
Form in the legs the pairs of
reverse folds shown.

11

Blunt the tips of the legs
with reverse folds.
Mountain fold the
body in half.

12

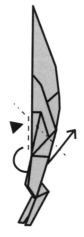

Reverse fold the legs
and hindquarters to the
right; the tail area will
automatically valley fold
itself in half as the reverse
fold is formed...see step 13.

13

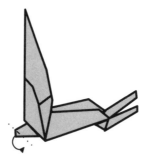

Shape the tail with a reverse fold.
Repeat on the far side of the tail.
Rotate the rear half of the white hart
to the position shown in step 14.

14

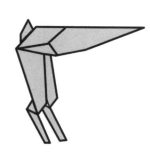

Completed rear half
of the white hart.

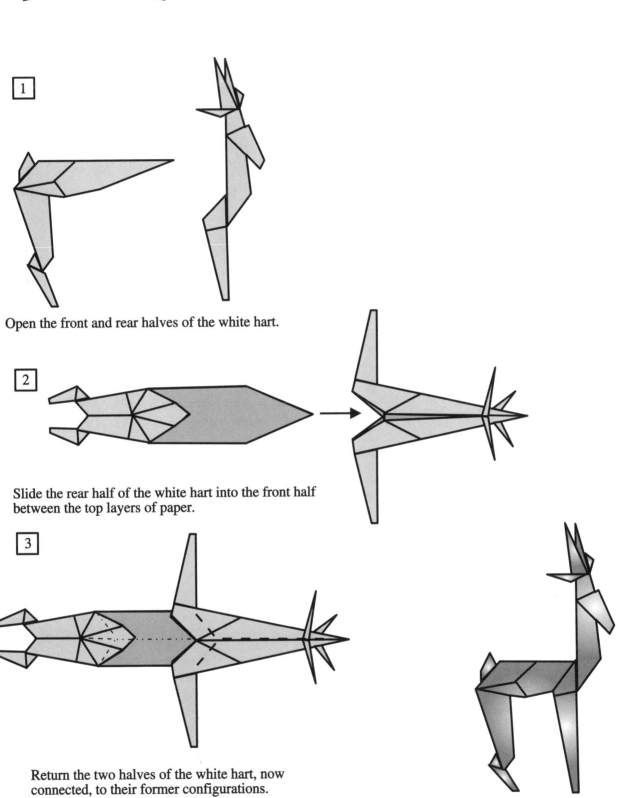

1

Open the front and rear halves of the white hart.

2

Slide the rear half of the white hart into the front half between the top layers of paper.

3

Return the two halves of the white hart, now connected, to their former configurations.
No new creases are made.

King's Hound

Fold the king's hound from two 3″ square sheets of paper.

1

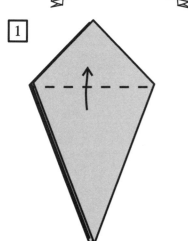

Begin with a bird base.
Valley fold the near flap up.

2

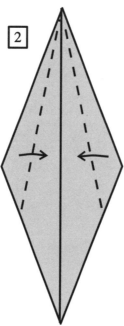

Valley fold the
sides of the top flap
to the centerline.

3

Reverse fold
the bottom
flaps outward
as far as they
will go.

4

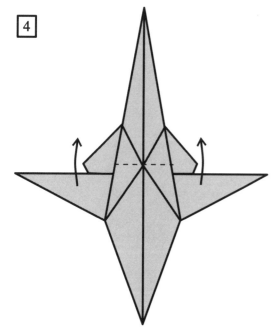

Valley fold the near lower
flaps upward.

5

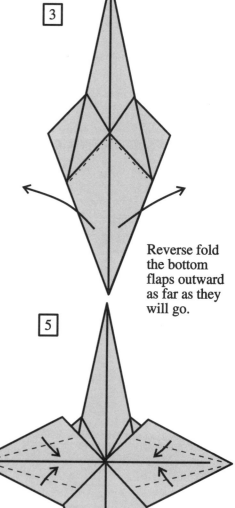

Valley fold the sides of the top flaps
to the centerline.

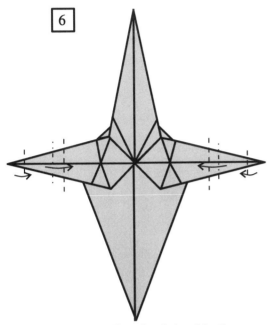

Valley fold the small ends of the side flaps.
Pleat the two side flaps as shown.

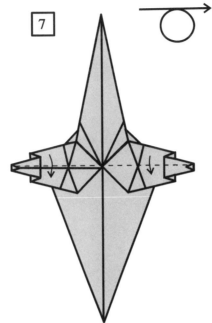

Valley fold the two
near flaps back down.
Turn the model over.

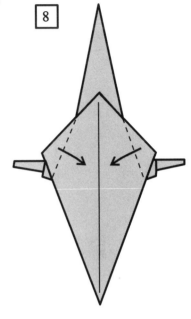

Valley fold the sides of the near
flap towards the center as shown.

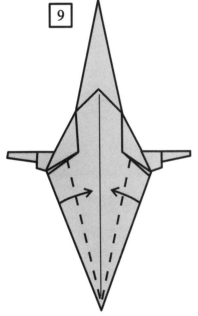

Pull the outer edges of the left half
of the near flap to the centerline
and flatten. Repeat on the right
half.

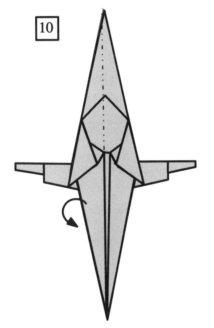

Mountain fold the
paper in half.

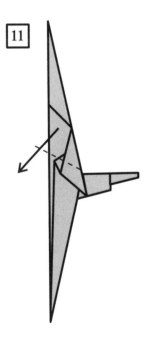

Outside reverse fold to
the left as shown.

12

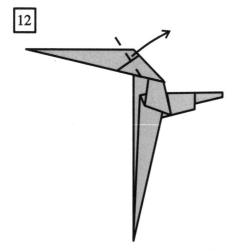

Outside reverse fold the top flap
on the diagonal as shown.
Turn the model to look like step 13.

13

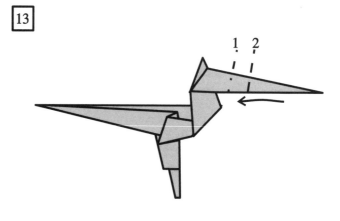

Form the head by making in order the
indicated reverse folds.

14

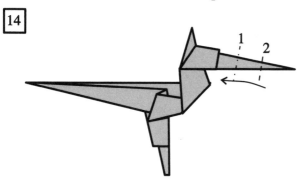

Form the muzzle and lower jaw
with two reverse folds.

15

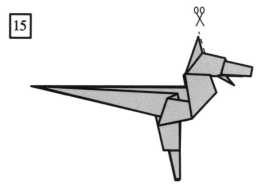

Slit the top flap to form two ears.

16

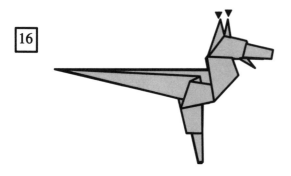

Squash fold open the two ears.

17

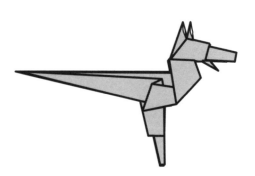

The completed front half of the hound.

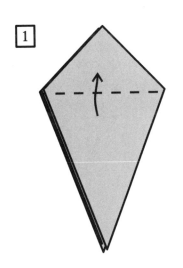

1

Begin with a bird base.
Valley fold the near flap up.

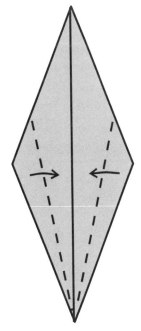

2

Valley fold the sides
to the centerline.

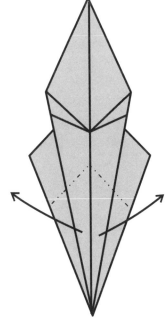

3

Reverse fold the bottom flaps
out.

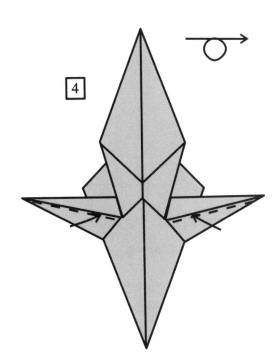

4

Valley fold the lower edges
up into the flaps
Turn the model over.

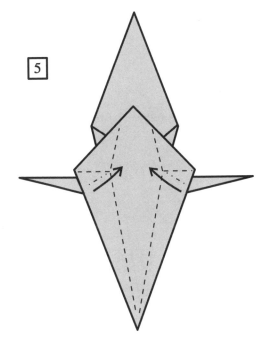

5

Working from the bottom, valley fold
the edges to the centerline; bring the
outer corners toward the center and
flatten them into the collars shown in step 6.

6

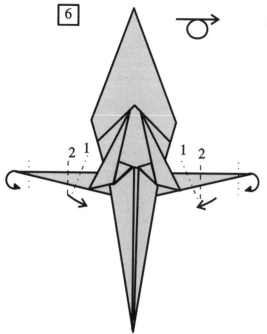

Blunt the tips with reverse folds.
Then shape the legs with pairs of
reverse folds.
Turn the model over.

7

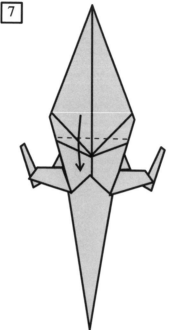

Valley fold the top flap down
as far as possible.

8

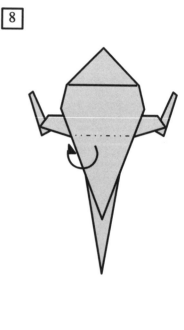

Mountain fold the near flap
up inside the paper.

9

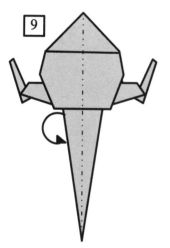

Mountain fold the paper in half.
Turn the model to the position
shown in step 10.

10

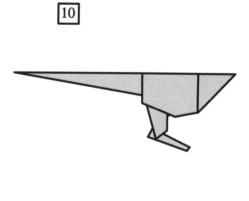

The completed rear half of the hound.

1

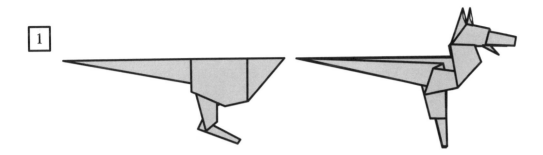

Open the front and rear halves of the hound.

2

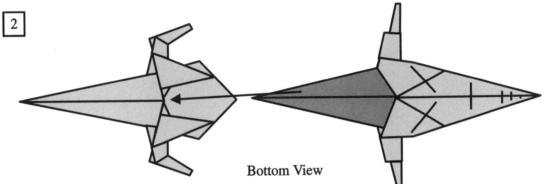

Bottom View

Slide the front half of the hound between the near layers of the rear half. (The right point of the rear half slides under the shoulders.)

Adjust the finished model by making a crimp at the base of the tail.

3

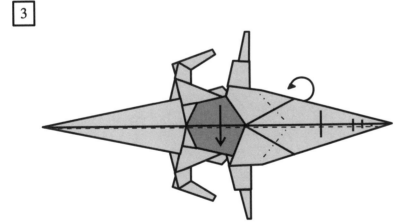

Valley fold the front and rear half of the hound along the centerline of both models.
Mountain and valley fold both front and rear halves to their original shape.

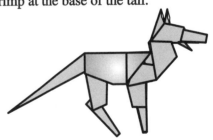

The flap on the top of the hound is a quilted pad to protect the hound from injury during the hunt.

Longbow

Fold the longbow from a 2″ square sheet of paper.

1

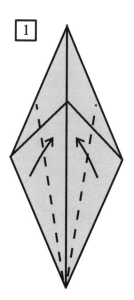

Begin with a fish base.
Valley fold the sides to the centerline.

2

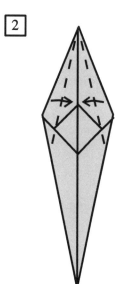

Valley fold the sides to
the centerline.

3

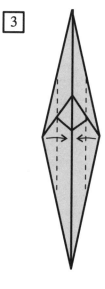

Valley fold the sides to the
centerline.

4

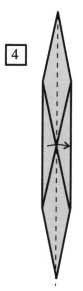

Valley fold the paper in half.

5

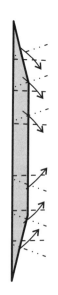

Crimp the paper to bend
the longbow.

6

The completed longbow.

Crossbow

Fold the crossbow from a 2″ square sheet of paper.

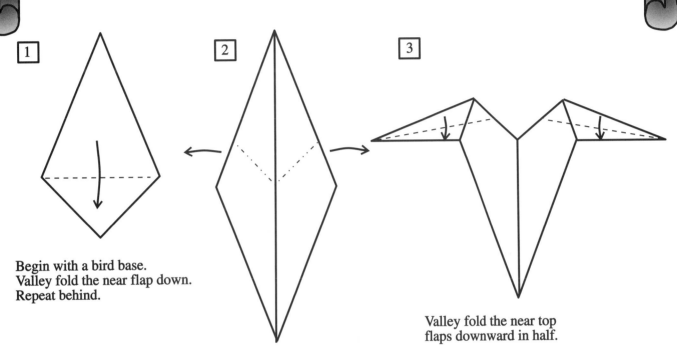

1

Begin with a bird base.
Valley fold the near flap down.
Repeat behind.

2

Reverse fold the top flaps out
as far as possible.

3

Valley fold the near top
flaps downward in half.

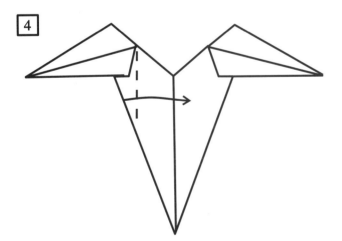

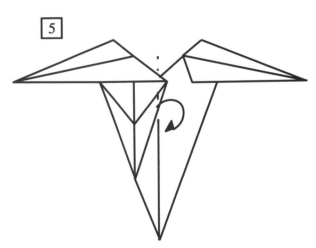

4

Pull the left edge free and
flatten it all the way to the
right; continue the valley
fold downward parallel to
the centerline.

5

Mountain fold the new right edge
inward along the vertical centerline.
Repeat steps 4–5 on the right.

6

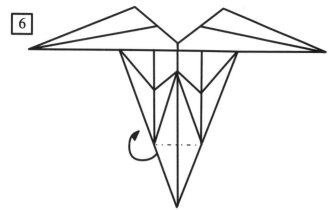

Tuck the bottom point of the
near flap up inside the model.
Repeat steps 3–6 behind.

7

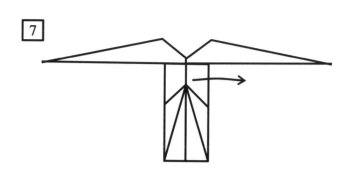

Open out the right lower flap
without unfolding the bow.

8

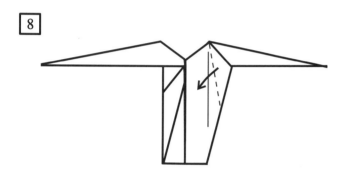

Valley fold the near right edge of the paper
along the diagonal as shown.
Mountain fold the side flaps down as you
valley fold the model in half on the centerline.

9

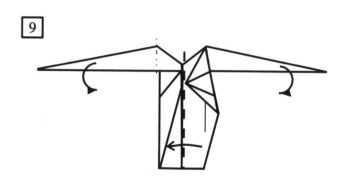

Mountain fold the side flaps down as you
valley fold the model in half on the centerline.

10

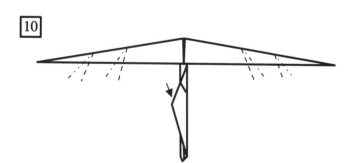

Crimp the side flaps to bend the bow.
Mountain fold the near flap
down into the outside pocket
on the side of the crossbow.

11

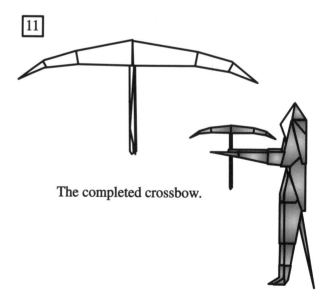

The completed crossbow.

Handcart

Fold the handcart from a 6″ square sheet of paper, its handle from a 6″ x ½″ rectangular sheet of paper, and its wheels from two 3″ square sheets of paper.

Cart

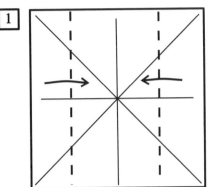

1

Begin with an unfolded waterbomb base. Valley fold the sides to the centerline.

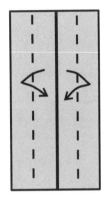

2

Valley fold the center edges to the outside folded edges and return them to the center.

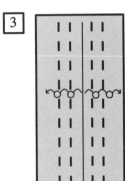

3

Valley fold the central edges to the creases made in step 2, and then fold these doubled edges outward, forming again the step 2 creases.

4

Mountain fold the paper in half.

5

Reverse fold the bottom corners inward.

6

Valley fold the sides to the centerline. Repeat behind.

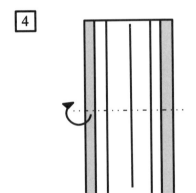

7

Valley fold the top flap down as shown. Repeat behind.

8

Mountain fold the bottom half of the flap up into the two small triangular pockets behind the flap. Repeat behind. Open up the model.

 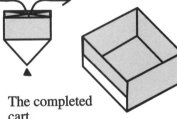

9

The completed cart.

  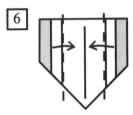

1

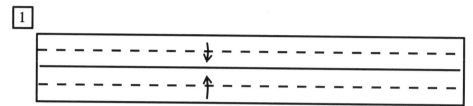

Valley fold the outer edges to the centerline.

2

Valley fold the paper in half along the centerline.

3

Valley fold the ends of the paper as shown.
Make two valley folds in the center of the paper.

4

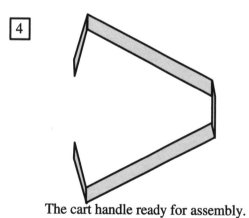

The cart handle ready for assembly.

1

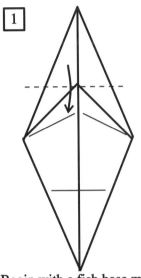

Begin with a fish base made from an unfolded waterbomb base. Valley fold the top down to the crease line made by the waterbomb base.

2

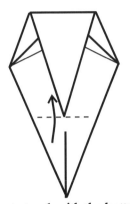

Repeat step 1 with the bottom flap; note that the waterbomb crease is no longer visible.

3

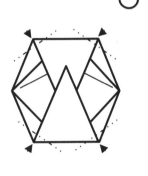

The paper should look like this. Reverse fold the four small corners into the paper. Turn the paper over.

4

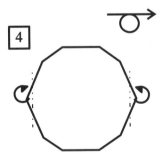

Mountain fold the two side points behind the paper. Turn the paper over.

5

The back of the paper showing where the flaps are located.

6

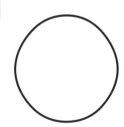

The finished wheel ready for the assembly.

1

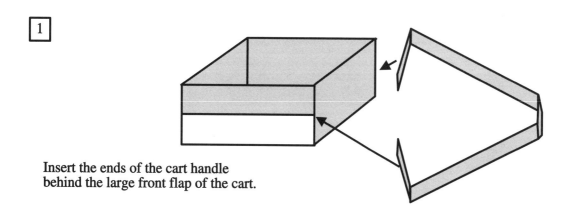

Insert the ends of the cart handle
behind the large front flap of the cart.

2

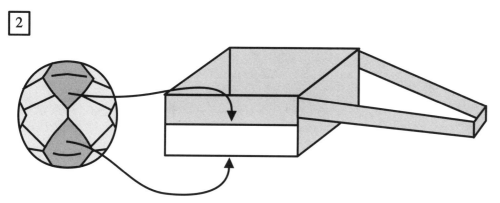

Insert the top flap on the back of the wheel
behind the bottom flap on the side of the cart.
You may have to shorten this flap if it is too
long. Insert the bottom flap on the back of the
wheel into the pocket on the bottom of the
cart. Repeat this assembly on the reverse side.

3

The Adventure Begins

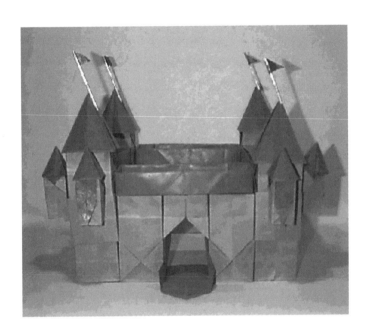

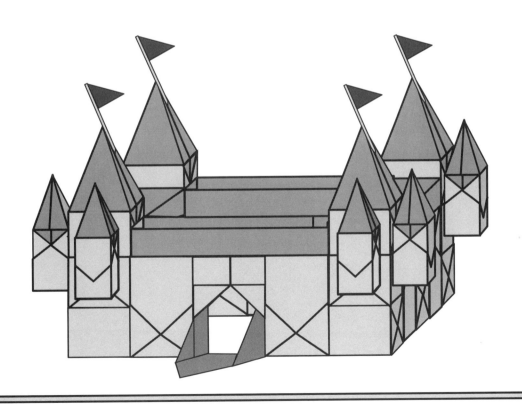

This book gives you an opportunity to fold any of the thousands of characters in the legend of King Arthur, but there is more to the adventure. Consider that the dragon has been created so that a pair of wings can be attached to its back. If you look closely at the horse, you will find these same pockets. In this way you can fold Merlin's flying horse. The possibilities are endless.

The possibility of creating characters of different sizes using proportional origami will allow you to make the giants, elves, and fairies you may have read about in the stories of King Arthur. Oberon, the king of the fairies, has a modified version of the dragon's wings. Gargantua's club is a modification of the knight's sword. Try your hand at creating these simple models.

Did fairies and elves ride on the backs of deer? Can you create a deer using the rear half of the horse to make a deer with the flap on its back? This is how you begin to design your own models, by experimenting with models you have learned. Ask yourself, what happens if I fold the paper a different way? If you want to create a deer with a flap like the horse, examine the way in which the horse was folded and assembled. Apply what you have learned to a new model.

The fairy tale castle and Camelot contain the necessary models for creating all of the castles found in the Arthurian legends. Take the castles and experiment with their different parts. The enchanted castle on the following page is just one of many you can create. These modular structures are interchangeable, and allow you to create an inexhaustible number of different castles. The adventure of folding begins with an idea and never ends.

These models make King Arthur's court come alive—the small squares of paper have turned into a magical kingdom. The folds have been kept as simple as possible, but these simple units have combined to form very complex origami structures. The knight with its horse, Merlin with his dragon, and King Arthur in Camelot are truly only the beginning.

The Enchanted Castle

The following models are needed to assemble the enchanted castle:
1 Camelot
1 fairy tale castle

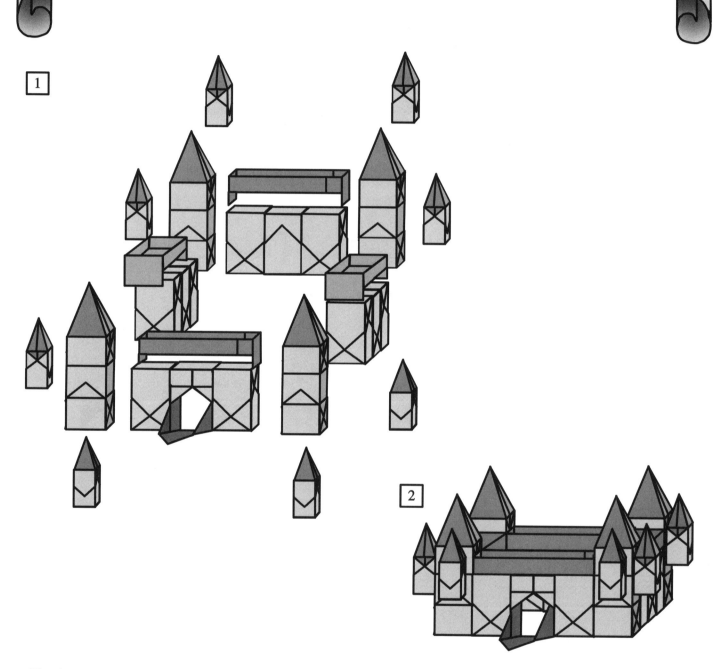

The drawings above show how to assemble the enchanted castle. First dismantle the fairy tale castle and Camelot. Step 1 shows how to assemble the enchanted castle from the walls, the ramparts, and the front of Camelot, and the towers and turrets of the fairy tale castle. Step 2 shows the completed model.

This should give you an idea of how to create other castles found in the legends of King Arthur.

Sir Lancelot

The following models are needed to assemble Sir Lancelot:
- 1 knight and sword
- 1 horse
- 1 jousting saddle
- 1 jousting bridle
- 1 Merlin's cloak made from a 3″ square sheet of paper
- 1 lance

1

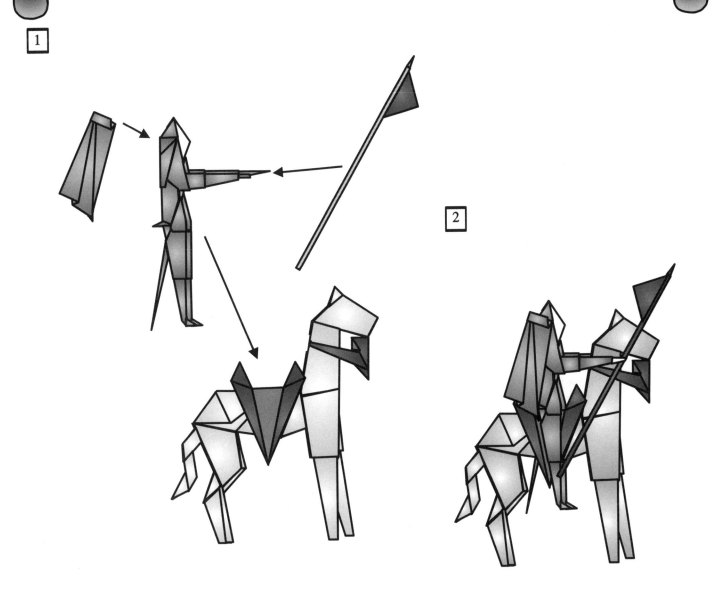

2

The drawings above show how to assemble Sir Lancelot. Lay out the models as they appear in step 1. The model of Sir Lancelot fits onto the horse in the same way as any of the knights. The lance can be held at an angle if you leave extra room when you fold the hand. Make a cape for Sir Lancelot out of a bright color paper. Slip it on the back of Sir Lancelot's neck. You may want to make the horse out of white paper. Step 2 shows the completed model.

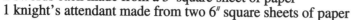

Gargantua

The following models are needed to assemble Gargantua:
  2 swords each made from a 3″ square sheet of paper
  1 knight's attendant made from two 6″ square sheets of paper

 1   2   3

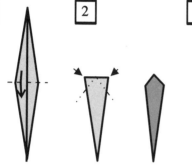

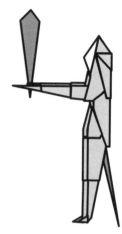

1 Unfold one of the swords to step 5 and valley fold the paper in half.
2 Reverse fold in the corners.
3 The giant's club complete.

Place the club in the giant's hand.

Elves

The following models are needed to assemble the elves:
  1 knight's attendant made from two 3″ square sheets of paper
  1 maiden fair made from two 3″ square sheets of paper
  2 eight-sided cones each made from a 1″ square sheet of paper

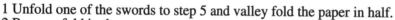

Place the small hats on the heads of the models. You may wish to
make a small staff out of a 4″ x ½″ rectangle.

Merlin's Magical Flying Horse

The following models are needed to assemble Merlin's magical flying horse:
  1 horse
  1 dragon's wings made from a contrasting color

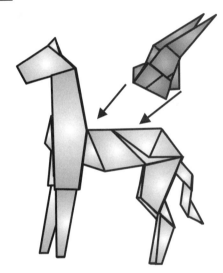

Place the wings on the back of the horse. Insert the square end of the wings under the back flap on the horse. Slip the front sides of the wings behind the outside layers of paper on the shoulders.

The completed model of Merlin's magical flying horse.

The Fairy King Oberon

Fold Oberon by making a knight's attendant from two 4″ square sheets of paper. Fold Oberon's wings from a 2″ square sheet of paper.

Oberon's Wings

1

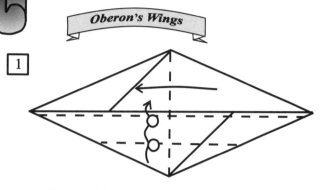

Begin with step 2 of the dragon's wings.
Valley fold the bottom flap up twice.
Then valley fold the paper in half to the left.

2

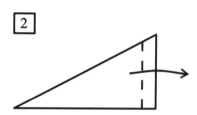

Valley fold the near flap as shown.
Repeat behind.

3

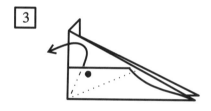

Squash fold the top flap down. The dotted line shows where the valley fold should form itself. Watch the black spot on the back portion of the flap.
Repeat behind.

4

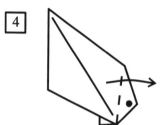

Valley fold the near wing from corner to corner as shown.
Repeat behind.

5

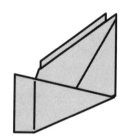

The completed model should look like this.

Assembly Instructions

Step 1 shows the model of Oberon with the back flap open.
Step 2 shows where to place the wings on his back.
Fold the back flap down.
Step 3 mountain fold the bottom of the flap under to hold the wings in place. Fold the wings back.
Step 4 shows the completed model of Oberon the Fairy King.

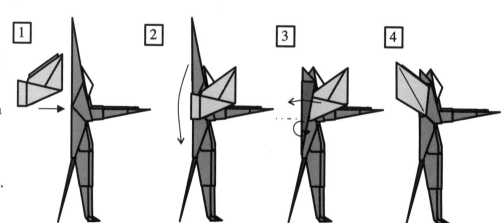

Proportional Origami

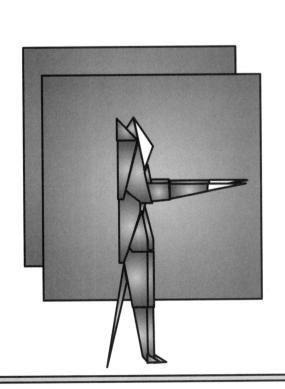

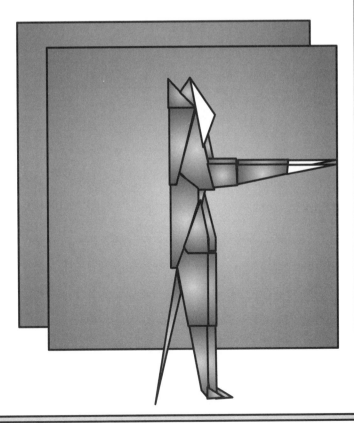

Proportional Paper

The following pages will show you how to make the models in this book from different size paper than that recommended, while still keeping the various models in proportion to each other. The process is a simple one, requiring no elaborate calculations.

First you must decide what size square paper you wish to use for the largest models: the fairy tale castle, the Round Table, the campaign tent, Camelot, Merlin's tower, and the enchanted castle, etc. If you wish your models to be larger than those in this book, then use paper larger than eight inches square; if you wish your models to be smaller, then use paper less than eight inches square. Keep in mind, though, that the smaller the paper, the harder it is to fold the models.

After you have chosen a base paper size, decide which model you wish to fold, note its recommended paper size, then turn to the proportional paper section dealing with that paper size. For example, if you wish to fold a knight (whose recommended paper size is 4″), turn to the page entitled Changing 4″, 2″, and 1″ Proportional Paper. This page will show you how to cut your paper to produce enough smaller squares to make two knights.

Be sure to fold all the models you wish to use from the same size base paper so that they will remain in proportion to each other.

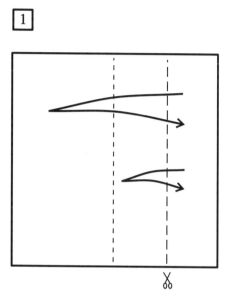

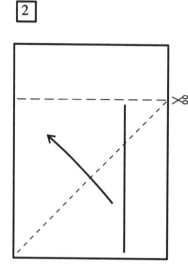

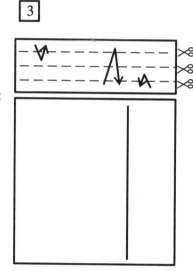

1

Valley fold and unfold the base paper in half. Valley fold and unfold the edge to the crease line. Cut the paper along the second fold line and discard the smaller piece.

2

Valley fold the paper on the diagonal. Cut the paper along the edge of the folded flap. You now have an appropriate size square for folding the horse and other 6″ models.

3

Valley fold and unfold the small rectangle in half. Valley fold and unfold the top and bottom to the centerline. Cut the paper along the crease lines. You now have four appropriate size rectangles for folding the lance and other 6″ x ½″ models.

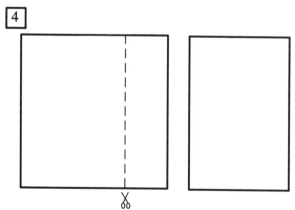

4

Cut the large square in step 3 along the crease line and discard the smaller piece. You now have an appropriate size rectangle for folding the throne back, or other 4″ x 6″ models.

1

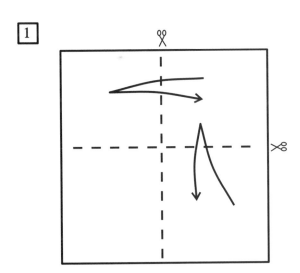

Valley fold and unfold the base paper in half. Valley fold and unfold the paper in half in the opposite direction. Cut the paper along the crease lines. You now have four appropriate size squares for folding the knight or other 4″ models.

2

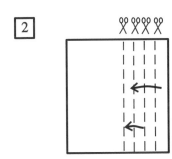

Valley fold the edge of one square made in step 1 to the centerline. Valley fold the newly formed edge to the centerline. Unfold all the folds. Cut the paper along the crease lines. You now have four appropriate size rectangles for folding Vivian's belt and buckle and other 4″ x ½″ models.

3

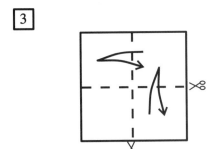

Valley fold and unfold the edge of one square made in step 1 in half. Valley fold and unfold the square in half in the opposite direction. Cut the paper along the crease lines. You now have four appropriate size squares for making the knight's sword and other 2″ models.

4

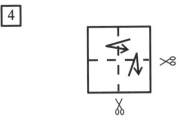

Valley fold and unfold one square made in step 3 in half. Valley fold and unfold the square in half in the opposite direction. Cut the paper along the crease lines. You now have four appropriate size squares for folding the elves' hats and other 1″ models.

1

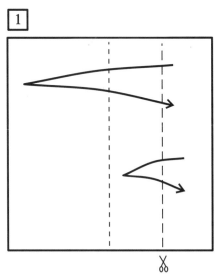

Valley fold and unfold the base paper in half. Valley fold and unfold the edge to the crease line. Cut the paper along the second fold line and discard the smaller piece.

2

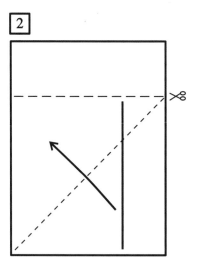

Valley fold the paper on the diagonal. Cut the paper along the top edge of the folded flap and discard the smaller piece.

3

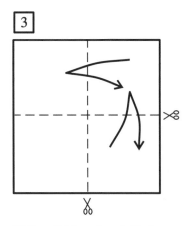

Valley fold and unfold the square generated in step 2 in half in both directions. Cut the square along the crease lines. You now have four appropriate size squares for folding the hound and other 3″ models.

4

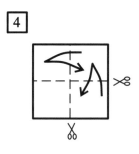

Valley fold and unfold one square made in step 3 in half in both directions. Cut the paper along the crease lines. You now have four appropriate size squares for folding King Arthur's crown and other 1½″ models.